ELECTORAL POLITICS IN FEDERAL INDIA

ELECTORAL POLITICS IN FEDERAL INDIA

MP Local Area Development Scheme

N.K. Sahu

GYAN PUBLISHING HOUSE
New Delhi - 110002

Electoral Politics in Federal India
MP Local Area Development Scheme

ISBN : 81-212-0901-3

Rs. 690

Published in 2006 in India by
Gyan Publishing House
5, Ansari Road, Daryaganj,
New Delhi - 110002
Phones : 23261060, 23282060 Fax : 23285914
e-mail : books@gyanbooks.com
website : gyanbooks.com

Laser Typesetting at : Vinayak Printers, Delhi
Printed at : Salasar Imaging System, Delhi

Dedicated
to my dear Father
who moulded me as a liberal human

Contents

Preface

For ages, the people in government have contributed to the growth and refinement of knowledge. Though the quality of such contributions varies, the public and readers commonly expect inside stories and perspectives of the development practitioners. And the expectations are higher whenever the writer is a serving bureaucrat and a specialist professional civil servant. But the readers are mostly left disappointed as sensitive issues are either not taken up or are inadequately dealt. Secondly, only in few cases scientific analytical tools and methods of social sciences are utilised to through scientific insight into the functioning of the matrix of social forces and its interaction with institutional and structural arrangements at a particular historical setup. Attempts have been made here to over come these deficiencies as far as possible. First, a subject has been chosen that is sensitive because of its' controversial nature. At the first instance, few might find the subject of the book, viz. analysis of a innocuous looking developmental scheme called Member of Parliament Local Area Development Scheme (MPLADS) not only monotonous, mechanical and run-of-the-mills but also too limited in its scope. But this scheme is probably the most sensitive and controversial amongst the hundreds of developmental schemes being implemented by the Government of India. This also is the most misunderstood one. Besides few structured studies, the scheme related information is mostly published and analysed in media. You would find hardly any supporter of this scheme, excluding off course, the Members of Parliament (MPs) themselves. Thus any attempt to write a full book on this topic should be seen as a courageous endeavour. The purpose is to bring out the important aspects of the scheme that are either neglected by social commentators, media and research scholars or are not covered adequately. Secondly, while descriptive narrative method is used to analyse the functioning of the scheme, a numbers of analytical tools and methods are also used to explain deep interactive systems.

For a brief period in 1998 and 1999, I got chance as a government servant to directly implement this scheme at the Government of India level. I was a main player in preparing the scheme guidelines, release of funds and monitoring it. In the process, chances to interact with hundreds of MPs and other stakeholders became common. During this period I conceptualise the analytical framework within which the scheme should be studied and analysed. After that I worked with a political boss- a cabinet minister for more than four years. And this is the time when I got exposures to field level realities; filtering of thousands of local/personal needs, prioritising them and executing them at community level. Interaction with all the stakeholders - the MPs, villagers, communities, bureaucrats, political actors and contractors gave lots of insights. During this time I became a participant observer. Discussion with hundreds of MPs and other stakeholders helped me not only in understanding of the functioning of the political processes at the grass-roots level but also gathering of information. Thus I am probably the only person who has seen the scheme's functioning both from the top as well as from the bottom most level. In this book, the readers would find ample evidence of my experiences.

This book is a product of long years of labour. I sincerely owe a lot to all those thousands of people, including the intelligent villagers and urban dwellers, who have helped me in understanding the scheme functioning as well as the socio-political environment that governs our behaviour. I place on record my gratitude to Dr. Rajkishor Meher, Shri Jual Oram, Jatindra Das, Dr. Sanjeev Kumar, Mainsh, Parminder, N.K. Sharma, Balram Gumasta, Leena Pradhan, Tapan Sahoo, P.C. Pratihari, Himansu Sahu, and others who helped me to complete this work. I acknowledge the valuable advice and suggestions made by my seniors, specially, Dr. P.V. Thomas, Shri J.K. Mohapatra, Prof. Gopinath Pradhan and Shri B. Brahma.

For ruthless combing of the entire manuscript and bringing it to a presentable shape, I owe a special debt to Dipesh Satpathi and Shri Kandarpa Sahoo. Sattaveesa, Shatakratu, Jyotsna and others helped me morally and physically to undertake this venture, for which, I thank them. Despite my sincere efforts, there might be mistakes and loopholes, for which, I might be excused.

Naba Krushna Sahu

July 2006,
New Delhi

1
Introduction

Year 1993, Pamulapati Venkata Narasimha Rao was the Prime Minister of the Republic of India and the Congress (Indira) was the ruling party at the centre. Though the Congress (I) won popularity in the Parliament (10th Lok Sabha) it took a few months to form the government, the house was precariously hung and the government unstable. Congress (I) headed by Shri Rao with 247 Lok Sabha seats was balancing its existence in the house having 20 unattached Members of Parliament (MPs); a category of MPs never known earlier or after the 10th Lok Sabha and eleven political parties each having a single MP. Defection, stabbing political mentors from the back and threatening to resign from the house at the drop of the hat was the prevailing norm during those days. During such an exceptional time a development programme called the Member of Parliament Local Area Development Scheme (MPLADS) was introduced. Since then, this scheme has been popularly known as the 'MP Fund' and we choose to prefer this name through out this book.

"The MPLADS, launched by the Congress government on December 23, 1993, was strongly opposed by the then finance minister Dr. Manmohan Singh. But the prime minister P.V. Narasimha Rao went ahead and announced the scheme, proclaiming it *the first step towards true development as it reflected the conceptual departure in thinking with regard to development at the formulation and implementation level*" (emphasis mine, George Iype in *The Rediff Special,* 18 Dec., 2000).

Why MP Fund Scheme?

A number of political commentators have tried to probe the motive behind such a scheme. Swapna Majumdar thinks, "the programme was initiated to deflect public attention from the allegation of corruption leveled against Rao" (Lucknow: An MP's Report Card, *HT*). The logic for introducing the scheme is different for M. Prakash when he wrote "The move to set up such a fund was spearheaded by Ram Naik...In the early nineties, it was Naik who suggested that the centre should follow the example of the A.R. Antulay government and provide discretionary funds to legislators. What helped matters was the fact that a minority government, run by P. V. Narasimha Rao, was at the helm then and it needed all the goodwill possible to survive" (Withering Development, *Hardnews*, Oct., 2003). Some others think Rao, drew inspirations from his home state Andhra Pradesh. Members of Legislative Assembly (MLAs) used to recieve some funds from the Rural Development Department for constituency development in the early 1990s. The MPs complained that the MLAs were becoming popular and powerful with Central government money and so MPs should also receive similar funds. Narasimha Rao took a stand. The details of the operation of the MLA Local Area Development Scheme, as executed in different states, can be studied from Annexure II. This would help compare the MP Fund scheme with the MLA Fund scheme.

Provocative Words

The MP Fund Scheme has been a much discussed topic since its inception. One can hardly find a commentator who has written a few good words in support of this scheme. Some times the comments have been too harsh. A few examples:

- Flawed scheme: Strong case for scrapping MPLADS (news caption).
- Funds for legislators unconstitutional (V.S. Gopalakrishnan, *The Hindu*, ND, 3 Feb., 2004).

- More evidence that MPs development fund goes to big black hole (Ritu Sarin, ND, 18 April).
- Entirely against the letter and sprit of Constitution (73rd Amendment) Act. (*The Hindu*, Online edition, 3 Feb, 2001).
- Amendments have been introduced in the scheme, thereby substantially increasing the scope of corruption (M. Prakash, *Hardnews*, Oct. 2003).
- Two crores too much for MPs to keep track of (Sujata Dutta Sachdeva and Gurmukh Singh, *ToI*, ND, 2 March, 2001).
- Wastage by our representatives (Prem, *TIE*, ND, April 2001).
- A Fund for the Needy... or the Greedy (Neena Vyas, *The Hindu*, ND, March 2003).
- The expenditure under the scheme has been largely concentrated on projects, which inherently involve elements of corruption and misuse (Mohanti, 2004: iii).

Most Misunderstood

Majority of Indians - those who live in villages and mofussil areas, those who are uneducated and live at subsistence level – best appreciate the scheme. They are the people who cast vote in elections and also demand support - mostly financial of MPs, MLAs and other peoples' representatives. They want to utilize this fund for their community, village and locality. But, on the other hand, educated people and the enlightened political and social analysts are found to be the most confused section of our society. Only three examples will suffice to highlight the level of misunderstanding regarding the MP Fund Scheme.

- Completely unfettered discretion (Joginder Singh, former Central Bureau of Investigation director in *Asian Age*)
- Every thing under the moon (Why don't we get angry any more? While each MP was given a laptop computer as part of the MPLADS when it was launched by P V

Narasimha Rao to keep the flock happy,....says Krishna Prasad)

- Very little public accountability (What makes MPLADS every politician's dream-come-true is the fact that there seems to be very little public accountability over its use, writes M Prakash in *Hardnews*, Oct. 2003)

Both Joginder Singh and Krishna Prasad are wrong. Neither the scheme is under the MP's unfettered discretion nor can everything under the moon be funded through it. Like any other development and welfare scheme implemented by the government, the MP Fund Scheme too has design, execution and monitoring flaws. That does not mean that the funds are at the disposal of the MPs like the *khazana* (treasury) of the medieval kings. As per the existing financial procedure, the stipulated amount goes to the district collectors/magistrates in installments. The district collector/magistrate is also responsible for the execution of the works following due procedure, accounts keeping and submitting of periodic reports, including utilisation certificates. If any work is not allowed as per the guidelines, the district collector/magistrate has the power to reject the MP's suggestions, with proper justification. In a number of cases, the MP's request for allotting MP Fund to a particular type of work is not accepted either by the District collector/magistrate or the competent authority. A small list of such 'rejected requests' is given below:

- Hearses and mobile buses (Vijay Goel, MP, 13th LS)
- Dental van (N. K. P. Salve, MP, RS)
- Garbage collection van (Ramakant S Angle, MP)
- Saplings for special forestry (Jaysinghrao Patil, MP, 13th LS)
- LPG cylinders to poor women (Ram Naik, MP, 13th LS, while he was the Petroleum Minister)
- Pooling of funds for big projects (Eduardo Faleirio, MP, RS)

The accounts of the MP Fund scheme are subject to audit scrutiny. The Comptroller and Auditor General of India audited the scheme in 1998 and 2001. The Programme Evaluation Organisation of the Planning Commission evaluated the scheme in 2000. Lastly, the electorates do the most important audit exercise during the voting time.

Salient Features

The MP Fund scheme is a special category development and welfare programme. Four of its specific features are discussed below in brief.

(1) In the hundreds of development/welfare schemes implemented by the government, funds are released based on the progress made in its utilisation/expenditure. The MP Fund Scheme is an exception to this: the central government releases funds solely based on the progress in sanctions order. The district collector/magistrate intimates the total sanctioned amount out of total released funds and the government releases the next instalment based on some norms.

(2) In all other schemes, the unutilized/unspent amount at the end of a financial year lapses, but not so in MPLAD scheme.

(3) The direct beneficiaries and stakeholders in all other schemes are remotely consulted for scheme concepts, implementation procedure, monitoring system and financial outlays. But in MP Fund scheme, the primary stakeholders - the MPs - are consulted at every stage and on each aspect of the scheme. Rather they determine everything, though in a collective manner. Mostly separate committees on MPLADS of the Lok Sabha and the Rajya Sabha do this.

(4) Rigidity in scheme format and execution method is the hallmark of most of the development and welfare schemes, but not the MP Fund. Almost every year the MPLADS guidelines are changed in order to accommodate the operational and stakeholders' requirements. Annexure I gives in detail the changes that were incorporated in the scheme. The annual allotment of funds for each MP increased from a small

ANNEXURE: 1.1

MPLADS Guidelines: Consistency in Flexibility

Objectives:

February 1994

- Execution of small works of capital nature as suggested by the MPs based on the locally felt needs

December 1994

- The works under this scheme shall be developmental in nature based on locally felt needs

November 2005

- MPs may choose some works for creation of durable assets of national priorities namely drinking water, education, public health, sanitation, and roads under the scheme.

(Locally felt needs with in national priorities?)

Salient Features:

February 1994

- Works worth Rs. 1 crore per year
- Cost of individual works should not exceed Rs. 10 lakh
- Works should conform to the general pattern of programmes and projects within the District Plans and the Centrally Sponsored and Central Sector Schemes operation within the district
- Lok Sabha MPs would spend in respective constituencies. Rajya Sabha (RS) MPs may select any district from the state which he/she has been elected for exercising the choice of works

December 1994

- The nominated RS MPs may select any one district in any State/UT for implementation of their choice of works

September 1995

- Elected members of RS can choose one or more district(s) from the state of their election. Nominated RS MPs can select one or more District(s) but within one state of their choice
- Individual works costing more than Rs. 10 lakhs can also be taken up
- Funds to be released each year immediately after vote on account/budget, but based on actual progress in expenditure
- Whenever there is a change in the MP, the works identified by the predecessor MP that are under execution should be completed
- Also works identified by the predecessor MP pending sanction beyond a period of 45 days from the day of recommendation by the MP, are also to be executed

February 1997

- Allocation of Rs. 1 crore per year under the scheme is for the constituency
- The MPLADS fund is non-lapsable
- If the predecessor MP has not identified any work at all, allocation or releases of funds to such predecessor MP will not be additionally given to the successor MP over and above the entitlement

(Conformation to the District Plan dropped)

Financial year 1998-99 onwards

- Increase the allocation to Rs. 2 crores per year
- Interest accrued on funds deposited with the nationalized banks may be used for MPLADS works
- Unspent balance left by the predecessor RS MP will be distributed amongst the successor RS members in that particular state

(December 1998: Prime Minister's statement in the

- District collector to ensure maintenance of the works from the funds of local bodies or the relevant agency.
- District collector to refer the works to the concerned agencies/departments/organizations in the district for sanction and implementation.
- District collector to inspect at least 10% of works, so also the implementing agencies.
- Works should be completed in one or two working season.

December 1994

- Sharing and supplementing of MPLADS funds with funds from other sources not allowed.

September 1995

- Part funds can be used for completion of other larger works, provided it would result in completion of the works and it should be with reference to clearly identifiable part of the work.
- The time restriction on completion of works removed.
- Even for costly works (more than Rs. 10 lakhs) full and final power of sanction is delegated to the district functionary so that decision making is only at district livel.
- Sanction for work be accorded within 45 days.
- Implementing agencies may not collect administrative, centages charges, etc., for their services.

February 1997

- Reputed non-govt. organization allowed to implement the works.
- Signboards carrying the inscription "MPLADS WORK" may be prominently erected at the work sites.

Financial year 1998-99 onwards

- Each installment of Rs. 50 lakhs will be released as soon as a statement indication the unsanctioned balance below Rs. 50 lakhs is received from the District Collector.

February 1999

- A time limit is to be stipulated for completion of work depending upon the merit of each case.

April 2001

- MP or his representative and the Nodal officer or Collectors are to be present at the time of distribution of funds to executing agents.

February 2002

- Allow the District Collectors to utilize half per cent amount as contingency expenditure out of the annual allocation of MPLADS.
- Signboards carrying the inscription "MPLADS WORK" with the name of MP may be permanently and prominently erected at the work sites.

February 2004

- MPs of 13th Lok Sabha may be continued to be associated as Ex-MPs with the functions relating to their MPLADS projects even after dissolution of the Lok Sabha and till the Code of Conduct, to be announced by the Election Commission, takes effect.

November 2005

- Each MP will recommend works up to the annual entitlement during the financial year preferably within 90 days of the commencement of the financial year in a prescribed format to the concerned District Authority.
- The work and site selected for the work execution by the MP shall nao be changed, except with the concurrence of the MP concerned.
- If the commitment for the full estimated amount is not forthcoming and the amount recommended by the MP is less than the estimates for the work and there are no other sources from which the deficit can be made, then the work should not be sanctioned.

- Purchase of night soil disposal system for local bodies
- Purchase of motor boats for flood and cyclone affected areas

February 2004

- Construction of bar (legal practitioners) library

November 2005

- The illustrated list of permissible works deleted

Illustrative list of non-admissible works:

February 1994

- Works which do not fall within the scope of the district plan
- Office building
- Works belonging to commercial organizations, trusts, registered societies, private institutions, added or cooperative institutions
- Repair and maintenance works
- Grants and loans
- Memorials
- Purchase of inventory or stocks
- Acquisition of land or any compensation for land acquired
- Assets for an individual benefit
- Place of religious worship
- Completion of incomplete schemes

December 2003

- Substitution of public contribution with MPLADS funds not allowed in any Central/State programme which includes a component of such contribution

November 2005

- All renovation and repair works except heritage and archaeological monuments and buildings

- Purchase of all movable items except vehicles, earth movers, and equipments for hospital, educational, sports, drinking water and sanitation purpose belonging to Central, State, UT and Local self Government (this will be subject to 10% of the capital cost of the work for which such items are proposed)
- All revenue and recurring expenditure
- Works within the place of religious worship and on land belonging to or owned by religious faith/group

ANNEXURE: 1.2

Members of Legislative Assembly Local Area Development Seheme (MLALADS): Salient Features As On December 2003

Year of Introduction	*Amount of Funds (Start & Present)*	*Objectives*	*Special Features*
Delhi: MLA Local Development Scheme			
1994-95	Start: Rs. 1.00 crore Present: Rs. 1.40 crore	Small works of capital nature: strengthening and augmentation of infrastructure facilities	• MLA to write to MDC/NDMC for works amounting to Rs. 70 lakhs and to Urban Development Deptt. of Rs. 70 lakhs per year. • No duplication of works covered under Plan scheme and MPLADS (certificate is to be furnished). • There is a 'permissible' and 'not-permissible' list of works.
Maharastra: Local Development Progra mme of Legislators			
1984-85	Rs.65 lakh (1998) MLA MLC & Nominated legislated	Local development programme of the legislator on local need	• The concerned MLAs should propose 90% works and the other members of the Dist. Planning and Devp should propose remaining 10% works. Board • Maximum limit of exp. Per work is 10 lakh but for Kilhapur type embankments it is Rs.15 lakhs. • The Display Board does not permit writing of name of the Legislator.

Contd ...

Table Contd ...

			• MLA can propose construction works for the areas affected by calamity/disaster outside their constituency, an amount of Rs. 5 lakh per year from the recommended list.
Uttaranchal: Vdhayak Nidhi Yajana			
1998-99 as part of Uttar Pradesh	Present: Rs. 50 lakh	Local development programmes.	• Very similar to the Bidhayak Nidhi Yajana of Uttar Pradesh. • There is a permissible (20) and not-permissible (9) list of works. • Release of funds: 35% first quarter, 15% second quarter, 35% third quarter and 15% fourth quarter. • The amount is kept by the District Magistrate in the PL account.
Chattishgarh: Chattishgarh Local development Scheme			
The Legislative Assembly Development Scheme was replaced by the Chattishgarh Local development Scheme in the year 2002	Not specified (demand driven)	Development of local areas, small works.	• District Collector is the nodal officer at the district level. • Any other peoples' representatives may also give proposal. • The cabinet would approve. • The Collector would decide the implementing agencies. • Funds are released in two to three instalments • Money is allotted as per the nature of the works. • There is a permissible and a not-permissible list of the works.
Bihar: Vidhan Mandal Sadasya Vikas Yojana			
1997	Not specified (Demand driven)	Local area development	• Proposals from the Vidhan Mandal Sadasya will be sent to the Deputy Development Commissioner (DDC). • The proposals would only be for their circle development works. • There is a list of permissible (33) and not-permissible works.

Contd ...

Table Contd ...

			• Within a month the proposal should be recommended by the DDC. • Books, furniture, etc. Allowed.
Gujarat: Community Works of Local Importance (MLA Grants)			
1989-90	1989-90: Rs. 10 lakh 1990-91 and 1991-92; Rs. 5 lakh 1992-93: Rs. 10 lakh	To enable the MLAs to accomplish minor works of the nature of missing links in their relevant constituencies.	1. **Discretionary Provision**: District Planning Board sanction 100% amount of the expenditure. 2. **Incentive Provision** : 1) works costing Rs. 60,000 without peoples' contribution 1005 funded by the MLA; 2) works costing mare than Rs. 60,000, peoples' contribution up to the tune of 10%, 25% and 50%. • 33 nos. of schemes can be taken-up only under Incentive outlay out of 96 schemes. • Rest 62 nos. of schemes can be taken-up from Incentive and Discretionary outlay. • Submit detailed proposal to District Collector. • No case doll. • Only government agencies implement. • Consonance/not in consonance list of schemes/works.

Assam (Rs. 20 lakh), **Rajasthan** (Rs. 60 lakh). **Nagaland** (Rs. 10 lakh), **Orissa** (Rs. 5 lakh) and **Tamil Nadu** (Rs. 82 lakh).

No MLA Local Development Scheme or any equivalent or the scheme Goa, Mizoram, Himachal Pradesh and Haryana.

2
Rationale and Logic of MP Fund Scheme

Millions of years back the size of the brain tripled in one primate species, the *Homo Sapiens*. His conscious activities based on intelligence are controlled in the cerebrum, the largest part of the brain, comprising gray matters. Therefore all human action, except reflex action, are supposed to be rational and logical. Recall how Mr. Hercule Poirot, the eccentric and egotistic detective character in Agatha Christie's stories, solved a number of complex murder mysteries by using the gray matter. Similarly, limited and scarce resources are utilized to achieve maximum gains. Now the question is, does the government have a brain to act rationally to provide benefits to the citizens? The logic of having the MP Fund scheme was described in the introductory chapter. Now it is time to examine the internal logic of the scheme.

From a utilitarian perspective, an action is morally right if it results in greater happiness for the greater number of people. In a welfare state, the government engages itself in various activities to provide comfort to its citizens. Government spending in the United States is about 30 per cent of the gross domestic product and in continental Europe, it is about 45 per cent. The figure is 17 per cent in India. But one thing is common to all these countries: they introduce every government action, i.e., taxing the citizens, subsidising necessary consumption or erecting big dams and factories, after justifying its rationale in terms of internal logic, external environments and the means and resultant benefits. A bureaucratic and mechanical method is followed by the government at the time of introducing a scheme as per preset conventions. At the outset it may appear uninteresting, boring, dull and monotonous, but, if we use our gray matter to analyse its internal logic, it becomes lively and enlightening. Let us engage ourselves in the exercise of finding the internal logic of the MP Fund Scheme, first following the conventional method, and then, by a modern tool, called the 'Logical Framework' method.

EFC/SFC/CCEA/Cabinet Note

Procedure is important, but, when it gets precedence over the rationale and results of an action, the outcome becomes substandard. There are hundreds of examples where government-run schemes and projects are introduced and implemented under a suffocating environment of demand for adherence to procedure. The philosophy is, if you follow the right path, the end would always be good – good for greater number. This is mostly similar to the Gandhian approach to 'Karma' in contrast to the stand taken by Machiavelli, where the end justifies the means. Without indulging in the merits of these lines of approach to scheme/project/programme implementation, we may say that, the Govt. of India follows a detailed procedure for formulation, appraisal and approval of government funded projects. But the reality is different. The project/scheme formulation and appraisal have been an *ex-post* exercise rather than an *a-priori* one. This means, the decision to start a particular scheme is done by the political executive and subsequently the bureaucratic executives roll the procedural web to justify the decision of the political boss. There is nothing wrong with this, as, the people's representatives are supposed to know the well being of the people and the society. What is worrisome is the weak implementation of the schemes and projects. Let us analyse the official thinking that goes into the project preparation process.

The government does admit that the additional time and effort spent at the project formulation and appraisal stage is worth it and results in qualitative improvement in terms of final project impact. A project is introduced only after following all the steps that are supposed to make it a success. Feasibility report (FR) is made by the administrative ministry/department to get in-principle approval of the Planning Commission. Then, the Detailed Project Report (DPR) is prepared for inter-ministerial consultation. There is clear-cut delegation of powers for project appraisal and approval. Aspects of time frame, applicability, evaluation, capacity building and time and cost overruns are given due weightage while launching a scheme. The DPR is prepared within the context of national, sectoral and sub-sectoral priorities, strategies and policy framework. The DPR specifies the project objectives, target beneficiaries, project strategy, legal framework, environmental impact assessment, ongoing initiatives (to avoid duplication and establish synergy), technology issues, management arrangements, means of finance and project budget, time frame, risk analysis, evaluation, success criteria, financial and economic analysis and sustainability. On the basis of the DPR, note for the Cabinet, Cabinet Committee on Economic Affairs (CCEA), Expenditure Finance Committee (EFC), Public Investment Board (PIB) and Standing Finance Committee (SFC) are submitted for approval. The aim of all these paper work is to make the scheme a success by analyzing every aspect. But, this is not the case with the MP Fund scheme. The due procedure was followed only after a decision was taken to go for such a scheme, though; the managerial, social and technological aspects were pushed in to the background.

The Logical Framework

Logical Framework is a tool used by project planners. International funding agencies like United States Agency for International Development (USAID), World Bank (WB), Asian Development Bank (ADB), Department of Foreign Aid and Development (DFAD), and Oxfam. use it while launching a new project idea. Though it is not a standardise tool, and is used in a discrete manner, its popularity is gradually increasing. This is because of its capacity to capture the whole project structure and functions within a single framework and the beauty of sorting the internal logic of the project components in a hierarchical and interconnected manner. This tool is also flexible and accommodating in nature while applied to even the most complex projects as well as simple ones. Again, it can be utilized in case of not only projects but also even to schemes, programmes (garland of schemes) and macro plans. Logical Framework specifies three more things: (a) the monitoring and evaluation mechanism that is to be followed during the project life, (b) the responsibility and obligations and (c) the rights of all the stakeholders and project managers.

Logical Framework is a popular device for consensus building but criticized for neglecting the institutional environment. "For example, logical framework analysis is based precisely on the isolation of casual links (e.g. input-output-impact) from the institutional contest. It provides an instrument for generating public consensus, and is able to do so to the extent that it identifies a common ground of agreement and relegates differences (underpinned by a range of political and institutional objectives) over which agreement may be difficult under the label of 'assumptions'- i.e. influences beyond management control. May be the fictional notion of simple casual links between designed inputs and outputs is absolutely necessary to the consensus building which moves planning forwards, but it only removes from visibility the agenda to which arguments over design relate." (Mosse, 1998: 50)

Logical Framework or simply log-frame is a matrix having four columns and four rows. All the 16 cells are logically interlinked to each other in one way or other. The logic can be established either vertically or horizontally, in isolation or in combination. The analytical aspects of the log-frame captures the hierarchy of project objectives, the causal linkages within the hierarchy, the underlying important assumptions and risk factors, and, lastly the notion of hypotheses and theories. Log-frame concept can be well understood by studying the Figure 2.1 and 2.2 that discusses the example of cooking Indian recipe- *Biryani*, a *Mughal* recipe.

Biryani is one of the most popular Mughal recipes of South Asia. The common variety is mutton *biryani*, a wholesome meal

Figure: 2.1 Logical Framework Matrix

	Narrative Summary	*Objectively Verifiable Indicators (OVI)*	*Means of Verification (MOV)*	*Important Assumptions and Risks*
⇑ ⇑				
V	1	2	3	4
E R T	Goal	Measure of goal achievement	Source of information and the method used to collect it	
I	**DEVELOPMENT PROGRAMME HYPOTHESIS**			
C A L	Purpose	Final result of end product	Source of information and the method used to collect it	Assumptions affecting purpose-goal linkage
	DEVELOPMENT PROJECT HYPOTHESIS			
L O G	Outputs	Quantity and quality of output	Source of information and the method used to collect it	Assumptions affecting outputs-purpose linkage
I	**IMPLEMENTATION HYPOTHESIS**			
C ⇑	Inputs	Quantity and quality of inputs	Source of information and the method used to collect it	Assumption affecting inputs-outputs linkage
⇑	⇒ ⇒ **HORIZONTAL LOGIC** ⇒ ⇒ ⇒ **HORIZONTAL LOGIC** ⇒ ⇒ ⇐⇐⇐⇐ ⇐⇐⇐⇐ ⇐⇐⇐⇐			

of exotic flavor and aroma. Our project is to prepare this recipe and learn the method of utilising logical framework to understand the mughal culinary art (Figure 2.2).

The Vertical Logic

Indicates the hierarchy of project objectives and the means to achieve them based on a number of assumptions and theoretical and practical knowledge. It starts from the bottom and moves upward step by step. If we cook the **inputs** like rice, mutton, refined oil, onion, Indian curry powder, etc following a particular culinary method, it will result in Mutton *biryani* - the **output**. Cooking the Mutton *biryani* is not everything. It should be well flavoured and testy. Thus the **purpose** is to cook a *Mughlai* recipe that is not only tasty but also attracts with exotic aroma. Lastly, the project succeeds, only when the purpose results in achievement of the wider **goal** of achieving satisfying the consumers.

Inputs result in output, output results in purpose and purpose results in goal depending on a number of assumptions. This vertical hierarchy of assumptions is identified in the last column. For example, marinating the mutton mixed with all

Figure: 2.2 Logical Framework of Biryani Cooking Project

Narrative Sum mary	*Objectively Verifiable Indicators (OVI s)*	*Means of Verification (MOV)*	*Important Assumptions*
1	2	3	4
Goal Satisfaction	Consumers grade the preparation	Opinion of consumers	
Purpose Well flavoured, good testing *Biryani*	Near by surrounding get attracti ve aroma Testy to mouth	Consumption/ eating	The flavor and ta ste is good, quantity is sufficient and other side recipe are also available
Output Mutton *Biryani*	3 kg. Mutton *Biryani*	Physical measure of quantities	Appropriate art of cooking is applied
Inputs Mutton Rice Refined oil Onion Coriander powder Turmeric powder Red chili powder *Garam masa la* Curd Cloves, Cardamom Salt Cooking fuel Cooking Vase Deep Frying pan Time	1 kg. Mutton cut to small pieces, 500. gm basmati rice, 250 gm refine oil, 1 kg. Onion, 100 gm. coriander powder, 20 gm. turmeric powder, 20 gm red chili powder. 100 gm. *garam masala*, 200 gm curd, 10 cloves, 20 gm salt, LPG for 1. 5 hour, Thick flat based cooking vase (8 inch deep, 10 inch diameter), Deep frying pan (3 inch deep, 10 inch diameter), 2 hour marinating time, ½ hour rice cooking time, ½ hour cut-onion frying time, 1 hour mutton preparation time, ¼ hour mixing and final preparation time.	Physical measure of quantities Quality of ingredients when purchas ed from a reliable grocery	½ hour cooking of rice would make it soft but not sticky. 2 hour marinating of mutton mixed with masala (coriander, red chili, tamarind, garam masala) in curd would make the mutton tender and flavored. ½ hour deep frying of cut - onions would make onion pieces red and crispy. ¾ hour preparation of marinated mutton in low heat and ¼ hour in high heat would dry the water but cook the mutton soft. Mixing of cooked rice, mutton and fried onion and preparing in low heat for ¼ hour result s in the final recipe.

masalas (coriander, red chili, turmeric pest/powder, etc.) in curd for two hours will make the mutton tender and flavored. These assumptions along with few more are required to provide the proper environment to transform inputs to output. Similarly, it is assumed that the cook knows how to cook *biryani to ensure good taste* while transforming the output- *biryani* into 'purpose'. The consumer would be fully satisfied only when the assumption that the taste is good, quantity is sufficient and other side recipes (*Kuchumber* - curd water mixed with little pieces of onion, green chili and coriander leaves) are available side by side.

The casual link between the inputs and output, output and purpose, and purpose and goal is based on the vertical hierarchy of hypothesis, theory and practice. In this case, the inputs (rice, mutton, etc.) would transform into output (*briyani*) only when the theory and practice of *biryani* preparation is known to the cook.

The Horizontal Logic

"The objective of the horizontal logic is the measurement of the resources and results of a project, through the identification of Objectively Verifiable Indicators (OVIs) and Means of Verification (MOV) for these indicators" (Coleman, 1987: 256). As highlighted by Coleman, these OVIs as identified in the second column are important, plausible, sufficient and independent in order to make them objectively verifiable. In the *biryani* preparation project, for inputs the OVI are one kg of mutton, half kg of Basmati rice, 250 grams of refined oil, etc. as listed in the log frame matrix. The OVI for the output is 'three kilograms of *biryani*'. The log frame also mentions about the means of verification (third column) that unambiguously identifies the source and the method of information (OVI) collection. For example, the quantity of ingredients must be measured physically at the procurement point and in the kitchen before put to the cooking process. The OVI and MOV capture the monitoring and evaluation mechanism of the project.

The Logical Framework of the MP Fund Scheme

In the previous sections, it was mentioned that the MP Fund scheme was introduced before the internal logic of the scheme is examined critically. Like all other government run projects/schemes and programmes, first the scheme was launched by the political executives and then the guideline were prepared by the ministerial executives. And, it was left to the general public and academics and journalist to find out the rationality of the scheme. We have done exactly the same here. The scheme is put to the rigor of analytical scrutiny as per the log-frame method now only, though this tool is prescribed for use prior to introducing a scheme. However, this ex-post exercise (Figure 2.3) is carried on only to find out the complex mosaics of the scheme's internal logic.

1. *The Vertical Logic of the Narrative Summary*

The objectives of the scheme, as mentioned in the guidelines issued from time to time by the government, are the

Figure: 2.3 Logical Framework of MPLADS

Narrative Summary	Objectively Verifiable Indicators (OVIs)	Means of Verification (MOVs)	Important Assumptions
Goal • Development and welfare of local areas and constituencies.	• Change in the district development indicators (economics, social, infrastrure, empowerment)	• District statistical abstracts and hand books (Qt. & Ql.)	
Purpose • Creation of durable assets of developmental nature based on locally-felt needs. • Bridging the gap between the locally felt needs a nd resources /provisions of other schemes, programmes and plans.	• Total value of assets created • Additional assets created (value) over and above through other schemes (ratio, %)	• Annual District report on MPLADS (Qt. & Ql.) • District statistic al abstract and hand book (Qt.) • Field survey, evaluation (Qt.& Ql.)	• The durable assets created supplement but do not substitute the assets created by other developmenta l schemes, programmes and plans. • Sufficient quantities of soft ware (human and other) are available to fully realise the benefits of the assets created. • The durable assets/capitals created together with the outputs/ benefits of other schemes, projects, and programmes are sufficient.
Outputs • Buildings for school s, residential schools, hospitals, veterinary centers, libraries, and crèches • Construction of tube wells, drinking water tanks, roads, drains, gutters, pathways,	• Nos. of works • Value of assets worth Rs. 2 Crores pre year	• Assets register • Annual & monthly reports of the district authorities • Expenditure statements • Inspection reports of officers • Annual audit and evaluation reports	• The MPs are capable of detect ing the local needs. • The MPs are interested to prioritise the needs . • The assets created are durable and developmental.

Contd ...

Figure 2.3 Contd ...

bridges/ culverts, railway level crossings, bus - sheds/ stops, sports/cultural facilities • Farm/social forestry, horticulture, pastures, parks, gardens • Irrigation, drainage and desilting of ponds • Construction of non-conventional energy systems • Crematoriums and structures on burial/ cremation grounds • Hospital equipment, ambulance • Computers to school s • Works relating to animal care/welfare		10% of the works are to be visited by the District Collector/ district Magistrate	
Inputs • Financial resources • Human resources * Central agency * District agency * Field agency • Material resources	• Rs. 2 crores per MP per year • Release of Rs. One crore within 3 weeks after receipt of expenditure statement • Works sanction orders issued within 45 days • Works executed within 3 months after sanctioned • A team of 20+ staffs at New Delhi • DM/DC and staffs with a nodal officer in each district/ constituency (no extra and specific manpower) • State nodal department • Material resources of civil, electrical and of other nature in required quantity and quality	• Weekly funds release statement (DPI) • Annual/monthly report (DPI) • Expenditure statement (DPI) • Record books of District authority • Bank accounts and statements • Funds utilisation and progress reports	• Government policy is stable. • The Parliament, especially the Lok Sabha is stable. • The MPs willingly adhere to the MPLADS guidelines. • Planning and implementation schedules are weather and natural hazards adjusted. • Work execution is not influenced adversely by the party in power in the State. • Existing human resources are not only efficient but also sufficient.

main source of information based on of which the narrative summary of the log-frame is constructed. The spelled out objectives aim at executing of small works of capital nature as suggested by the MPs based on local needs, which shall be developmental in nature based on locally felt needs. The political and bureaucratic executives provide or mobilize the required 'inputs' (financial, human and material resources) and the district and sub-district level government agencies transform them into 'output'. The output mostly comprises fixed assets like buildings for schools, colleges and hospitals and infrastructure like roads, bridges and irrigation facilities. The scheme would be achieving a few objectives in developmental terms, or, would fulfill the 'purpose' of creation of durable assets of developmental nature based on local need. Secondly, it would also serve the purpose of bridging the gap between the local needs and the resources and provisions ordinarily available through other schemes, programmes and plans. The ultimate 'goal' of this scheme is the development and welfare of the respective constituencies of the MPs. All these scheme-objectives (inputs, output, purpose and goal) are causally linked.

2. *Notion of Hypotheses and Theory*

The causal linkages within the hierarchy of objectives (vertical logic) are established on the basis of hierarchy of hypotheses. In simple terms, each lower level objective is causally linked with its immediate higher-level objective based on a model derived from practical experience or theory. As depicted in Figure 2.1, the inputs are linked to the output on the basis of the "implementation hypotheses". The project managers have full control over output achievement, once the required inputs are made available. This is because there are a few external factors beyond project control and some of the actions involved are based on time-tested procedures. The causal link between the output and purpose is based on the 'development project hypotheses'. Some elements of uncertainty do exist at this stage of causal link. All these buildings, roads, bridges, irrigation facilities may not result in creation of durable assets of developmental nature based on local needs. Secondly, all these efforts may not be sufficient to bridge the gap between the needs and the available resources. Lastly, the 'development programme hypotheses' that establishes the causal link between purpose and goal is the most loose one and the uncertainty factor is the maximum. In this case, the creation of durable assets of developmental nature may not result in the achievement of the goal as there are many more external factors that determine the development of the local area and the constituencies of the MPs.

3. Important Assumptions

The log-frame of the scheme also explicitly identifies the important assumptions that affect the outcome in the vertical logic (narrative summary). These are the factors over which the project managers do not have any control. It is assumed that the inputs would result in the output, only when the government policy and the Lok Sabha (LS) are stable, the MPs willingly adhere to the MPLADS guidelines, the planning and implementation schedules have taken into consideration weather and natural hazards, and human resources are efficient and sufficient. The success or failures of the MP Fund scheme as pointed by the CAG, Programme Evaluation Organisation of the Planning Commission and independent studies can be explained logically, if we give a proper thought to the assumptions on which the success of the scheme depends. For example, the assumption of efficiency and sufficiency of human resources is not real. No additional staff is made available at the center, state and district levels to implement the scheme, and, the staff working on this scheme hardly receive any training. The stability of the Lok Sabha, as assumed for the success of the scheme, is also not fulfilled. The Lok Sabha along with its members changed four times since December 1993, when the scheme was introduced. The 10th LS lasted till 10 May 1996, the 11th LS lasted for a little more than 18 months (15 May 1996 to 4 December 1997), the 12th LS lasted for only 13 months (10 March 1998 to 4 December 1999) and the duration of the 13th LS was about four years (10 October 1999 to May 2004). Again, so for as the adherence to the MPLADS guidelines is concerned, the CAG has pointed out many examples of aberrations.

There are a few crucial assumptions behind the process of transformation of output to purpose. It is assumed that the MPs are not only capable of detecting the locally-felt needs but are also competent and interested to prioritise them as per developmental needs. As the elected representatives of the Parliamentary constituencies (LS), it is but obvious that they must be aware of the needs of their constituencies. But while prioritising the projects, the compelling developmental needs may not be put at the top of the list. This is reflected in the CAG findings - detected works that are beneficial only to religious sites. It is to be remembered that because of this nature of assumptions, the link between output and purpose is indirect and weak. If we move further up in the vertical logic ladder of the hierarchy of scheme objectives from purpose to goal, the linkages become much weaker. This is because of the dependence on more and more restrictive assumptions. The durable assets that are created should supplement but not substitute the scope of assets creation through other developmental schemes and programmes. These assets would not only be necessary, but also be sufficient to achieve the goal of development and welfare of the local area and the constituency.

4. The Horizontal Logic of the Objectively Verifiable Indicators

For each level in the vertical logic of the hierarchy of the objectives as shown in the narrative summary, there exist a set of objectively verifiable indicators that are based on the horizontal logic. These indicators are important, plausible, sufficient and objectively verifiable. The inputs are indicated specifically, like, Rs. 2 crore of financial resources per year per MP/constituency and the time frame within which this finance should move from top to the bottom (from centre to the implementing agencies and worksites). The OVIs also capture the exact provision of human and material resources that are made available for the scheme. Similarly the output is measured in terms of numbers of projects and the value of asset created annually. The OVI of the purpose is the total value of assets created and the additional assets created over and above those created through other schemes. This second OVI is required as the scheme is not supposed to substitute the efforts of other government schemes. Lastly, the OVI of the goal is captured by the positive changes that took place in the district/constituency development indices. When we move in the hierarchy of OVI from bottom to top, the indirectness and subjective nature of the OVI become obvious.

5. *The Means of Verification*

Each set of OVIs is suitably designed to get them collected as per a scientific method of collection and verification. The type of data to be gathered, the source of information and the technique of data collection is specified in the MOV hierarchy. In case of this scheme, the OVI corresponding to the inputs is to be collected from the weekly, monthly and annual funds release statement and the expenditure statements. This is to be done by the Department of Programme Implementation the center's executing agency. Record books of the district authority, bank account statements and fund utilisation and progress reports are MOVs at the district and sub-district level. The OVI of the output is collected from the assets registers, financial progress statements and the inspection reports of the field level officials, including the district collector. The above-mentioned two MOVs are available to the project managers. But for the two higher MOV, the data source is broad and sometimes is based on sample survey and field evaluations. Even qualitative elements of data type and method are introduced. Elements of aggregation problems do arise whenever the district and the constituency are not the same.

6. *Implications of the use of log-frame to MP Funds Scheme*

The exercise of putting the MP Fund scheme within the logical framework leads, as we can mark, to deep understanding of the functioning of the scheme. Now it becomes easy to explain the reasons for the under-performance or non-performance of the scheme as reported by the CAG and the Programme Evaluation Organisation. Now we know the internal logic of the scheme, which is based on a number of restrictive assumptions, unrealistic theories, hypotheses and a non-existent monitoring and evaluation mechanism. Regarding monitoring, the CAG is critical about the working of the Department of Programme Implementatio: "The Ministry's role, in effect, was confined to provide resources only without any responsibility for its use...clearly the Ministry failed to make much headway in ensuring that there was better utilisation of scarce resources it sanctioned for the MPLADS" (CAG, 2001). We have developed an ideal logical framework and come to know of the lacunae in the scheme by comparing the ideal with the real (Box 2.1).

Box: 2.1

Ideals	*Realities*
Assumption 1 : The government and the parliament are stable	Lok Sabha changed four times
Assumption 2 : The MPs and the officials adhere to the scheme guidelines	The guidelines are not followed properly
Assumption 3 : The implementing officials are efficient and sufficient	The implementing officials are neither efficient nor sufficient
Assumption 4 : The MPs are capable of Detecting local needs of their constituencies.	The constituencies are too big and diverse for a single person, i.e., the MP, to cover. Rajya Sabha MPs represent the state
Assumption 5 : The MPs are capable of prioritising the local need in developmental terms	Developmental priorities may not necessarily be the same as that of the vote capturing priorities
Assumption 6: The assets created are durable and developmental in nature	Non-developmental works like community halls, *mandaps*, religious places may also be taken up.
Assumption 7 : The assets created should supplement but not substitute the efforts of other schemes	Dovetailing with other schemes, projects and programmes is not possible as it falls outside the district and area plan mechanism (conformation to District plan dropped in February 1997 guidelines).
Assumption 8 : There will be no dearth of human and other resources to realize the full benefits of the assets created.	Even the maintenance expenses of the assets is not provided for in the scheme.
Implementation Hypothesis: The success of transforming the inputs into output to the fullest is based on engineering and management theories.	Field realities show that the local conditions may not be favourable. For example, the work cites are located in remote places, where the required raw materials may not be available or the land selected for use may not be free from litigations.
Development Project Hypothesis : The success of transforming the out put to purpose to the maximum extent is based on project managementheories.	The assets created may not be of the required quantity and quality
Development Programme Hypothesis : The success of fully transforming the purpose into goal is based on the theories of programmemanagement that explains the ways to combine multiples of projects, schemes and works	The risk of missing the target of goal achievement increases as all the projects and schemes implemented in a district are not conceptualised within an integrated plan framework
Monitoring Mechanism: The OVI and the MOV are scientifically specified within the logical framework of the scheme	The unorganised but effective political monitoring mechanism is not enough to overcome the weaknesses of the existing official monitoring system

The question is will the MP Fund scheme fail the way much-hyped schemes like the Training and Visit (T&V) system of agricultural extension and the *Warabandi* system in irrigation did?

Training and Visit System

The World Bank introduced the T&V system of agricultural extension in India and other countries. The three main assumptions of the system proved erroneous in practice. Robert Chambers (1997) identified them as the following:

- that representative contact farmers would be identified. (In practice they were usually better-off farmers);
- that a backlog of technology suitable for farmers was available, off the shelf. (This was rare)
- that agricultural extension staff would respond well to a regular routine and close supervision. (They did not)

Warabandi System

An irrigation water sharing system introduced in north-west India was later introduced all over the country. Robert Chambers (1997) observed:

For the system of timed shares to be feasible requires four conditions: clear land rights, stable water scarcity, channels to carry water to farmers' field, and a constant flow of water through a shared outlet. These conditions obtain in north-west India, where land has been adjudicated, there is little rain and so a stable shortage of water for much of the year, channels carry water to farmers' field, and, above all, canal systems have been designed to provide a constant flow day and night to groups of farmers. To find these four conditions combined elsewhere in India is rare indeed.

3
Stakeholder Analysis

The English physicist and mathematician, Sir Isaac Newton devised the laws of motion and gravitation that remained unchallenged for 230 years. His book *Principia* (1687) set out three laws of motion explaining the properties of forces and the relationship between force, mass and acceleration, and also the properties of gravity. He summed up one of the basic rules of the universe in the statement: Action and reaction are equal and opposite in nature. For example, the force that propels a shell out of a gun barrel (action) results in an equal and opposite force (reaction) of gun recoil. At a very superfluous level, a few principles in Hindu philosophy have some similarity with Newton's 3rd law of motion. The theory of *'karma'* has three principal meanings: (1) action, (2) consequences of actions and (3) destiny. "In its most popular form it states that there is a universal accounting system in which each individual must experience the consequences of all his actions (*karmas*); good action bring good result and bad actions inevitably result in suffering to the one who does them. The theory also states that the consequences of actions (also know as *karmas*) need not necessarily be experienced in the present life, they can be carried over into future lives" (*Be As You Are, The Teaching of Sri Ramana Maharshi,* edited by David Godman, Chapter 21: 210). Both in physical and metaphysical world, action and the actor must encounter the reaction and the consequences. Thus, if the actors know the probable results in terms of stakes, they are supposed to control or monitor their actions. Further, as God knows the in and out of the theory and practice of *karma*, He controls the destiny of the universe. Similarly, if we know the intention and action of all the actors in the functioning of the MP Fund scheme, it would be easy to predict the consequences of the scheme.

Eight principal actors have substantive stake in the MP Fund scheme. They are the MPs, the people of the constituency, the executives at the union, state and district level, the political parties, the political workers, the political representatives (MLAs, PRI representatives) and the works contractors and the order suppliers. In order to understand the functioning of the scheme, it is crucial to know the behaviour of different stakeholders. What factors they value the must while making a decision?

Analytical Framework

In order to understand the nature of the stakes of all these eight principal stakeholders we have tried to depict them in tabular and figurative analytical frameworks. In the tabular analysis, the stakes are measured in three types of relative scales. They are, (i) direct to indirect scale, (ii) private/personal to general/public scale, and, (iii) high to low intensity scale. A stake may be of direct or indirect importance to the stakeholders. It may personally benefit the stakeholder or may have some gains for the public. The third dimension is the intensity of the stakes in terms of benefits and costs. If the intensities are high, the location of the stake will be in one extreme, but if the intensities are low, the location would be in the opposite extreme. Table 3.1, 3.2 and 3.3 depict the location of the stakes of different stakeholders. Similarly, in the figurative analysis, the direct to indirect dimensions of the stakes are depicted in the vertical axis, the personal to public dimension of the stakes is depicted in the horizontal axes and the relative intensities of the stakes are depicted as circles. The bigger the sizes of the circles, the higher are the intensities of the stake and vice versa. The location of the circles explains whether the stake is directly or indirectly affecting the stakeholders or is personal or public in nature to the stakeholders. If the circle is located in the south-west corner, the stake is very private and directly available to the stakeholder. On the other hand, if the circle is located in the north-east corner, the stake is for the general public and it is very indirectly available to the stakeholders. We have drawn eight figures depicting the three dimensions of the stakes for the eight principal stakeholders.

Table 3.1: Stakes in the Scale of Direct-to-Indirect Accrual

Sl. No	*Stakeholders*	*Stakes (Benefits and Cost)* *Direct* ⇐ ⇐ ⇐ *Relative Distance* ⇒ ⇒ ⇒ *Indirect*
1	Members of Parliament	Political Goodwill · Well-being to Constituency · Pecuniary Benefits · Votes
2	People of the Constituency	Capital Assets
3	Executives (Central)	Better Equation with Legislatures · Non Pecuniary Benefits
4	Executives (District)	Careers · Relation with Politicians · Pecuniary Benefits
5	Political Parties	Political Goodwill · Votes · Developmental Works
6	Political Workers	Political Goodwill · Well-being of Local Area · Pecuniary Benefits · Votes in Local Election
7	MLAs & Panchayat Representatives	Political Goodwill · Well-being of Local Area · Votes in Election
8	Works Contractors & Order Suppliers	Pecuniary Benefits · Political Patronage

Table 3.2: Stakes in the Scale of Private/Personal-to-General/ Public Nature

Sl. No	*Stakeholders*	*Stakes (Benefits and Cost)* *Private/Personal* ⇐ ⇐ ⇐ *Relative Distance* ⇒ ⇒ ⇒ *General/Public*
1	Members of Parliament	Pecuniary Benefits · Votes · Political Goodwill · Well-being to Constituency
2	People of the Constituency	Capital Assets
3	Executives (Central)	Non Pecuniary Benefits Better Equation with Legislatures
4	Executives (District)	Pecuniary Benefits · Careers Relation with Politicians
5	Political Parties	Votes · Political Goodwill · Developmental Works
6	Political Workers	Votes in Local Election · Political Goodwill · Well-being of Local Area Pecuniary Benefits
7	MLAs & Panchayat Representatives	Votes in Election · Political Goodwill · Well-being of Local Area
8	Works Contractors & Order Suppliers	Pecuniary Benefits · Political Patronage

Stakeholder No. 1: The Members of Parliament

Borrowing the language of Abraham Lincoln, used in the context of 'democracy', we may say, the MPLAD is a scheme by the MPs, for the MPs and of the MPs. Naturally; the stake is

Table 3.3: Stakes in the Scale of High-to-Low Intensities

Sl. No	*Stakeholders*	*Stakes (Benefits and Cost)* *High* ⇐⇐⇐ *Relative Intensities* ⇒⇒⇒ *Low*
1	Members of Parliament	Votes Well-being of Constituency Pecuniary Benefits Political Goodwill
2	People of the Constituency	Capital Assets
3	Executives (Central)	Better Equation with Legislatures Non-Pecuniary Benefits
4	Executives (District)	Relation with Politicians Pecuniary Benefits Careers
5	Political Parties	Political Goodwill Votes Developmental Works
6	Political Workers	Political Goodwill Well-being of Local area Pecuniary Benefits Votes in Local Election
7	MLAs & Panchayat Representatives	Votes in Election Well-being of Local Area Political Goodwill
8	Works Contractors & Order Suppliers	Pecuniary Benefits Political Patronage

very-very high. The Indian Parliament and its constituents are constitutional institutions. Article 79 of the Constitution says, "there shall be a Parliament for the Union which shall consist of the President and two Houses to be known respectively as the Council of States and the House of the People". The Council of States, commonly known as the Rajya Sabha (RS) consists of 240 representatives, and, the House of the People, commonly known as the Lok Sabha (LS), consist of 550 representatives. The powers and privileges, of the houses of Parliament and of the members and the committees thereof is specified in the Article 105 of the Constitution. The Constitution provides that "there shall be freedom of speech in Parliament". These power and privileges of the Parliament and its members help in performing the legislative business of the government. However, with the introduction of the MPLAD scheme, the MPs got the power to perform some executive functions. Every year they are allowed to spend Rs. 2 crore on the development of their constituencies. The LS MPs implement projects within their parliamentary constituency, the RS MPs in the states which they represent and the nominated members throughout India. As the representatives of the people and the states, they are supposed to take care of the need of their constituents. Thus there is pressure on them to utilize the fund properly so that the voters are satisfied. Let us identify and analyse the 'stakes' in subsequent paragraphs.

Votes

To get re-elected to the Parliament is the prime objective of the MPs. The LS MPs try to appease the voters of their respective constituencies. Likewise, the RS MPs like to appease the MLAs and MPs who vote them to power. One thousand one factors determine the election results. We devote a separate chapter to explain all these aspects. However, our analysis shows that voters are remotely influenced by the utilisation of the MPLADS funds. Again, the RS MPs do not have any stake in this regard as the beneficiaries of the scheme do not directly elect them.

Pecuniary Benefits

Though sensitive, this aspect of the MPs' stake cannot be brushed aside below the carpet. The Indian media has been reporting many stories on kickbacks received by MPs in the MPLADS projects. In the 3rd week of December 2005, the Indian Parliament was rocked by TV sting operations showing some MPs accepting money in the 'cash for question scam' and 'cash for MPLADS works scam'. The Hindu, in its editorial wrote, "Just seven days after a sting operation exposed 11 MPs in a cash-for-question racket, another undercover investigation has caught seven more parliamentarians discussing kickbacks with television reporters for handing out contracts under the Members of Parliament Local Area Development Scheme (MPLADS). At another level, this investigation is further confirmation - if any were needed - of the corruption and vendality of those who occupy the highest legislative bodies in the country" (The Hindu editorial New Delhi, December 22, 2005). Similarly the Hindustan Times wrote "..MPs have a free hand to dole out contracts that have nothing tangible to show at the end. Part of the money mysteriously ends up in the pockets of the very MPs whose job it is to spent it on developmental work" (HT editorial, New Delhi, December 22, 2005). If we believe the late Rajiv Gandhi's view that the leakage in project implementation is as high as 85 per cent, one can very safely say that a part of that must be reaching the stakeholders. This would be more clear and apparent while we would, in subsequent sections, try to analyse the stake of the work contractors and order suppliers.

Well-being of the constituency

As the peoples' representatives of the parliamentary constituencies, the MPs are interested in the development and well-being of their constituents. This scheme was launched only to meet the demands of the public for small works of developmental nature. Prior to December 1993, the MPs were not in a position to provide financial help to meet the small requirements of the general public, like a narrow bridge connecting two or more human settlements or repair of a village school. Though they were the members of almost all the committees and forums that decide the developmental works in their constituencies/districts, the decisions were arrived collectively or jointly. Neither the benefits of these works were directly controlled by the MPs, nor were the credits for the works ascribed to them. But now with Rs. 2 crore at their disposal, the MPs are in a position to help and serve the constituency. The scope of the scheme may not be sufficient to meet all the demands of the people and the MPs are supposed to allocate the limited resources for the well-being of the constituency. They will have to prioritise the needs and derive the maximum benefits. The stake is high, so also the gain.

Political goodwill

The peoples' representatives are supposed to meet all sorts of demand of the people. Starting from the village panchayat representatives to the Member of Parliament, all directly elected representatives are in public service. Satisfaction of the voters is their prime responsibility. Voters need their help for various reasons - job, transfer, promotion, pension, social justice, protection from miscreants and developmental work. All these harvest political goodwill for the MPs. This may not result in winning an election, but, definitely wins the hearts of people. As elections are periodical, what is at stake is the maintenance of political goodwill with the help of the MP Fund Scheme. MPs are directly concerned about this.

All the stakes of an MP, as identified in the relative scale of (1) direct-indirect, (2) personal/individual-public/general perspectives and (3) relative intensity (Figure 3.1) are depicted below.

Figure 3.1: MPs' Stake in the Scheme

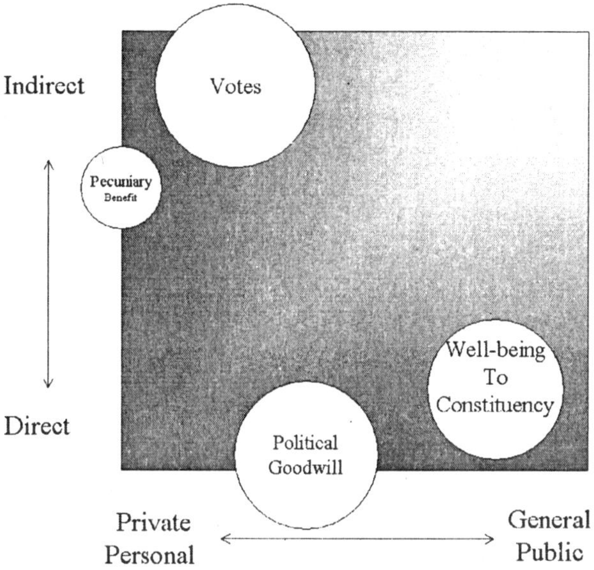

Stakeholder No. 2: The People of Constituency

The MP Fund Scheme is meant for the benefit of the constituency. The guidelines clearly spell out that the objective of the scheme is to execute small works of capital nature as suggested by the MPs based on local needs (February 1994 guidelines) and the works under this scheme shall be developmental in nature (December 1994 guidelines). As most of the territorial constituencies are undeveloped in terms of infrastructure, the funds available with the MPs under this scheme becomes useful for the local area development. The Programme Evaluation Organisation of the Planning Commission found that 30.78 per cent of the total fund is utilized for construction of roads and bridges, 22.89 per cent for community works, 19.00 percent for education and 11.78 per cent for drinking water and sanitation works (PEO, 2000: 18). Though, the constituency gets funds from a number of schemes for development of infrastructure, the works are mostly undertaken as per strict scheme guidelines (permissible/non-permissible works). In contrast, the MP Fund Scheme is highly flexible and the local population has a considerable say in the choice of the projects. The MPs, mainly the LS MPs, are amenable to pressure and lobbying.

All the stakes of the people of the constituency, as identified in the relative scale of (1) direct- indirect and (2) personal/ individual-public/general perspectives and (3) relative intensity (Figure 3.2) are depicted below.

Figure 3.2: Constituency People's Stake in the Scheme

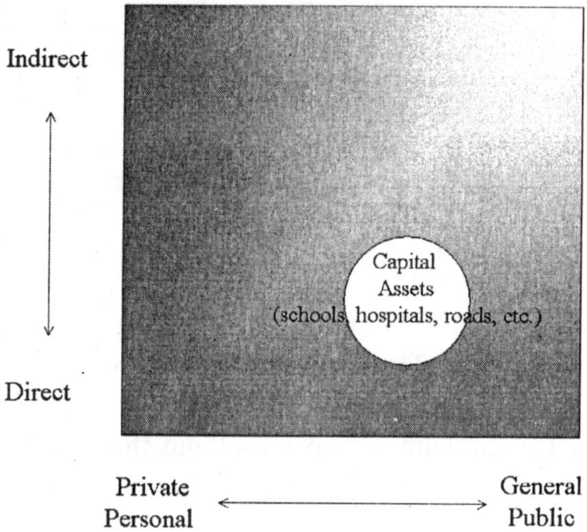

Stakeholder No. 3: The Executives at the Central Government

The bureaucratic executives at the central government release funds, monitor and evaluate the MP Fund scheme. The guidelines are prepared and the scheme executed accordingly. The size of the financial resources is also determined to a large extent at the union government level. Bureaucrats at the centre work to achieve the scheme objectives in a professional but impersonal manner. As they deal with 790 MPs, many of them ministers, it is but obvious that they work to the satisfactions of the MPs. The district administration seeks clarifications from the central executives whenever differences arise between the district collectors and the MPs. This gives some scope to them to get non-pecuniary benefit from both the parties (reservation of guest house, preferential treatment for darshan of deities/pilgrim places and confirmation of rail tickets). Political leaders and ministers are influential people. And everyone wants to have a cordial relationship with them. Thus, the central government executives also like to have better political equations with the MPs. Who knows they may get favour in terms of a ticket to the assemblies and parliament or nominations to commissions.

All the stakes of the executives of the central government, as identified in the relative scale of (1) direct-indirect and (2) personal/individual-public/general perspectives and (3) relative intensity (Figure 3.3) are depicted below.

Figure 3.3: Central Executive's Stake in the Scheme

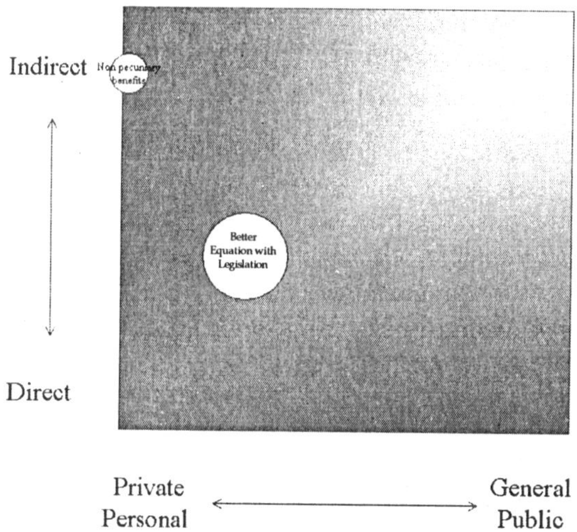

Stakeholder No. 4: The Executives at the District Administration

The district administration, especially the district collector/magistrate (DC/DM), play a crucial role in the implementation of the MP Funds Scheme. The MPs choose a particular district and its collector/magistrate as the nodal officer to execute and coordinate the activities of the scheme. They also convey the recommendations of projects in writing to the DC/DM. It is the responsibility of the DC/DM to examine the proposals as per the MPLADS guidelines and assign the work to different executing agencies. Officially they monitor the progress of project implementation and also keep the accounts and prepare reports for the use of MPs and central government. As the MPLADS guidelines only allow use of government agencies for execution of projects, most of the work goes to Public Works Department (PWD), block development officer (BDO), Public Health & Engineering Department (PHED), Rural Development Department and all other line departments. Of course the final work is done by the contractors. Because of these arrangements, the DC/DM and the line departments wield considerable power. The district administration and the officials want to have a cordial relationship with the MPs, as the latter are not only the representatives of the local people, but also powerful otherwise. There is scope of financial gain by the district and field officials as deciding the contract is in their hand.

Interaction between the MPs and the DC/DM improved after the introduction of MP Fund scheme. Both have funds at their disposal under multitudes of schemes, the MPs with (mostly) untied funds and the DC/DM with tied funds (many times more than the MPs). The results are:

(1) Exchange and swapping of projects between the MPs and the DC/DM. Even in a few instances, the DC/DM clubbed financial resources from different schemes with or without the knowledge of the MPs. "The DCs irregularly clubbed MPLADs funds (in 96 cases) with the funds of other schemes" (CAG, 2001: 9).

(2) Projects not covered under the scheme are recommended by the MPs and sanctioned for execution by the DC/DM.

(3) Executing agencies of choice of the MPs are accepted by the DC/DM, though there is no such compulsion under the scheme guidelines. For selection of executing agencies, 26% of DCs/DMs seek the advice of the MPs, 29% of DCs/DMs seek advice sometimes and 44% of DCs/DMs never sought advice of the MPs (PEO, 2000: 25).

(4) Sharing of other benefits (pecuniary and non-pecuniary).

Though common, the above types of collaboration and co-operation are not the rule of the day. "In an audit sample of eight States, the DCs incurred an expenditure of Rs. 3.97 crore on 370 works not recommended by the MPs,....This serious breach in propriety persisted despite similar mention in the CAG's Report of 1998" (CAG 2001: 14). Conflict between the MPs and the district officials is observed whenever the MPs' stake don't match with the administrative mechanism adopted by the DC/DM. The Times of India reported that "the process (utilisation of MPLADS funds) has not been smooth and MPs often find themselves at loggerheads with the district administration, which control the funds" (ToI, ND, 21 March, 2002). The Economic Times wrote, "as district magistrates enjoy overriding powers, the MPs have been cribbing that their proposals are not taken seriously. The first time MPs of the 12th Lok Sabha complained that virtually no projects were cleared due to continuing feud with the magistrates" (ET, 4 May, 1999). However, the three stakes that are identified are the determining factors for the sweet-and-sour relationship between the MPs and the district officials. This also determines the success of the scheme.

For officers, career is important. If they are from organised services like Indian Administrative Service and State/Provincial Administrative Service, career becomes far more important. Good results in achieving the scheme target and relations with politicians are a few factors that determine the career prospects of the officials. Instances of unauthorised activities to achieve career objectives are plenty. Because of the very nature of the MP Fund scheme, it becomes one of the most effective instrument in the hands of district officials to achieve career goals. The CAG reported that "the district collector of Beed, Pune and Satara went a step further. They invested Rs. 5.76 crore of MPLADS in small savings schemes to achieve their targets for the year 1999-2000" (The Times of India, 24 December, 2001).

All the stakes of the executives at the district level, as identified in the relative scale of (1) direct-indirect, (2) personal/individual-public/general perspectives and (3) relative intensity (Figure 3.4) is depicted below.

Figure 3.4: District Level Executive's Stake in the Scheme

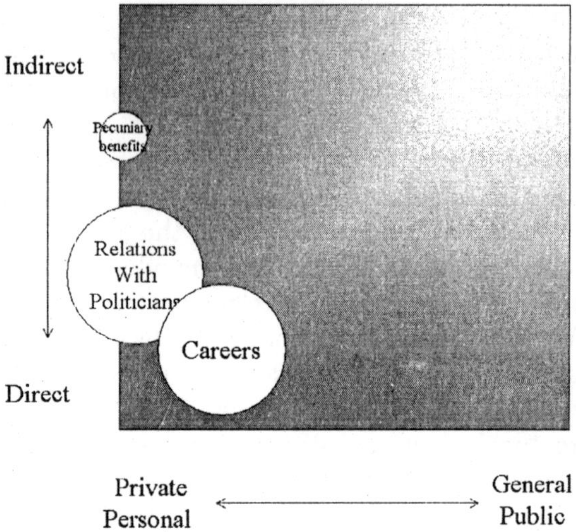

Stakeholder No. 5: The Political Parties

Keeping ideology apart, the main objective of the political parties is to capture power and rule. In a democratic republic like India, where people's representatives are elected to govern and legislate, political parties strive to mobilise human as well as material resources to capture power. They plan the 'vote bank' politics, and, in order to win elections at the federal, state and local levels, the MP Funds scheme becomes useful. Thus the stake of a political party in this scheme is to gain votes and political goodwill to the maximum possible and in remotely, development. In spite of high stake of political parties, there is hardly any evidence to conclude that they work to protect their stakes. There is no evidence to show that they educate and motivate their MPs and ticket aspirants in an organized and a systematic way to utilise this scheme to the advantage of the candidates, party and the people at large. An enquiry reveals that none of the national political parties keep any trace of the utilisation of the scheme funds meant for constituency development. The use of funds is found to be the personal responsibility of the individual MPs and the political parties hardly meddle in project implementation.

But off late it has been noticed that the political parties are also taking interest in MP Fund Scheme, indirectly for mobilizing financial resources. In March 2003 newspapers reported on Samajwadi Party's (SP) Mulayam Singh Yadav and Bahujan Samaj Party's (BSP) Mayawati levelling allegations of corruption against each other with regard to the scheme implementation. The SP gave a video cassette to the UP Governor Vishnu Kant Shastri, which allegedly proved that the BSP was diverting money to its own coffers from constituency development funds (ToI, ND, 5 March, 2003). In another development, UP Governor Vishnu Kant Shastri wrote to Chief Minister Mayawati, asking her to apprise him of facts of the cassette and CD controversy in which she allegedly told her party legislators to donate a part of their cuts from the "vidhayak and sansad nidhi" to the party coffer (ToI, ND, 6 March 2003). Mayawati launched a counter-offensive: "Mulayam will have to pay a heavy price for making false and fabricated allegations against me," Mayawati said, accusing him of accepting crores of rupees from the MLAs fund for a school named after his father (ToI, ND, 5 March 2003). These episodes indicate the involvement of political parties and MLAs/MPs in corruption by pointing out the stakes in terms of financial gains.

All the stakes of the political parties, as identified in the relative scale of (1) direct- indirect and (2) personal/individual-public/general perspectives and (3) relative intensity (Figure 3.5) is depicted below.

Parties are also taking interest in MP Fund Scheme, indirectly for mobilizing financial resources. In edly proved that the BSP was diverting money to its own coffers from constituency development funds (ToI, ND, 5 March, 2003). In another develto Chief Minister Mayawati, asking her to apprise him of facts of the cassette and CD controversy in which she allegedly told her party legislators to donate a part of their cuts from the "vidhayak and sansad nidhi" to the party coffer (ToI, ND, 6 March 2003). Mayawati launched a counter-offensive: "Mulayam will have to pay a heavy price for making false and fabricated allegations against me," Mayawati said, accusing him of accepting crores of rupees from the MLAs fund for a school named after his father

Figure 3.5: Political Parties' Stake in the Scheme

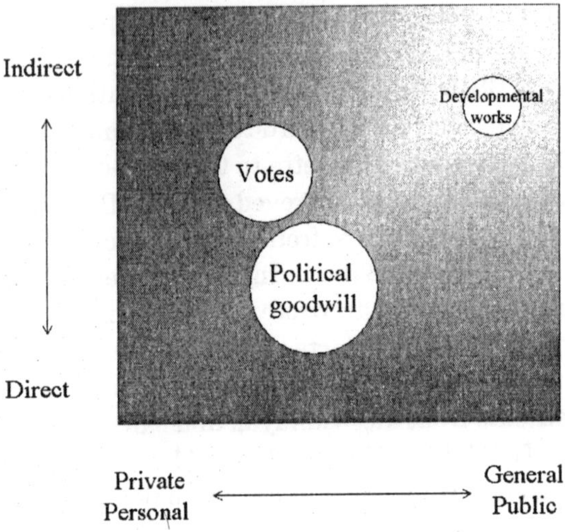

(ToI, ND, 5 March 2003). These episodes indicate the involvement of political parties and MLAs/MPs in corruption by pointing out the stakes in terms of financial gains.

All the stakes of the political parties, as identified in the relative scale of (1) direct- indirect and (2) personal/individual-public/general perspectives and (3) relative intensity (Figure 3.5) is depicted above.

Stakeholder No. 6: The Political Workers

Political workers are the backbone of political parties and the elected representatives in democratic polity of India. They are mostly citizens pursuing agriculture, business, industry, law and other professions. They have sufficient time to spare for party work. Ideology as well as other gains attract them to join a party and shift from one party to another. They are the grass-root agents who mobilize support for the parties and their candidates and play a crucial role in both general as well as local elections. Representing people in the panchayati raj institutions or having their own person elected is a key part of their ambitions. Though election results are determined by multiple

Figure 3.6: Political Worker's Stake in the Scheme

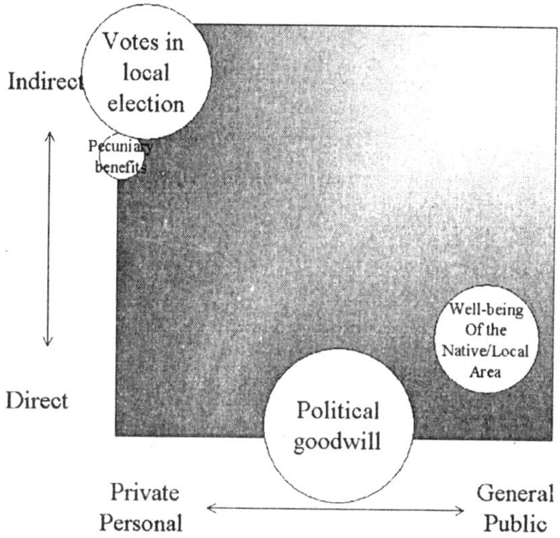

factors, using MPLADS projects to gain votes in the local election is common to all political workers. They are interested in the development of their area and pursue the elected representatives to undertake various developmental work and also try to help individual beneficiaries under a number of government schemes. They are closer to politicians than to government officials. Thus, the MP Fund scheme becomes very useful to them in achieving these objectives. Political workers also gain financially by acting as facilitators in the scheme implementation process. They play an important role in choosing the projects, executing agencies and the work contractors. And this results in some pecuniary benefits to them.

All the stakes of the political workers, as identified in the relative scales of (1) direct- indirect, (2) personal/individual-public/general perspectives and (3) relative intensity (Figure 3.6) is depicted above.

Stakeholder No. 7: The MLAs and the Panchayat Representatives

The PEO (2001) study found that "nearly three fourth of the works had originated from either the Panchayat Executives

Figure 3.7: MLAs and PRI Representatives' Stake in the Scheme

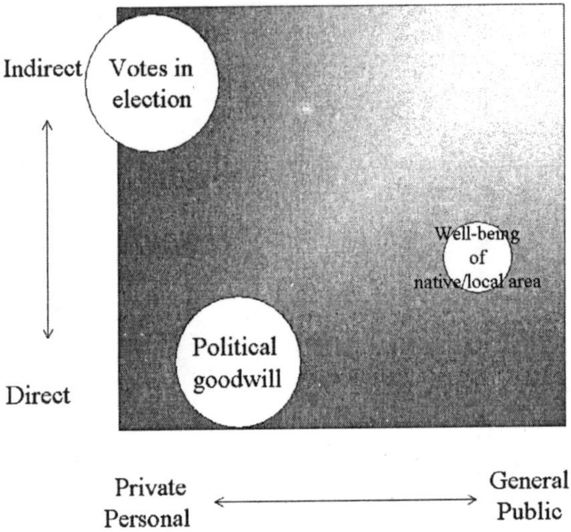

or the Municipal Councilors" (PEO 2001: 58). Being political activists, the MLAs and the people's representatives of Panchayati Raj Institutions (PRIs) and local urban bodies, have lots of stake in the MP Fund scheme. They have all the stakes similar to the MPs, political parties and the political workers. But the nature of their stake is unique - they operate within a competitive framework. The MLAs and the PRI representatives compete with the MPs to become politically more powerful. This is true for the same party MLAs and the representatives of the PRIs and obvious for the competing party candidates.

All the stakes of the MLAs and the Panchayat represantatives, as identified in the relative scales of (1) direct-indirect, (2) personal/individual-public/general perspectives and (3) relative intensity (Figure 3.7) is depicted above.

Stakeholder No. 8: The Works Contractors and the Order Suppliers

The MP Fund scheme allows construction works for creation of infrastructure facilities and purchase of items like ambulance, medical instruments, computers for schools and water tankers.

Figure 3.8: The Works Contractors' and the Order Suppliers' Stake in the Scheme

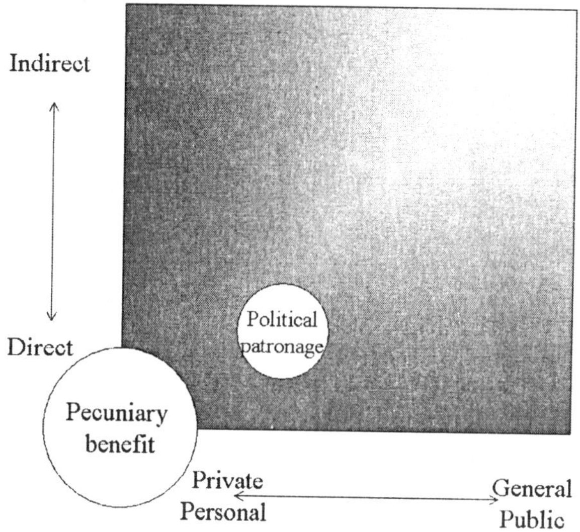

Though the MPLADS guidelines permit execution of projects only through government agencies, finally contractors and order suppliers come into the picture. The Programme Evaluation Organisation of the Planning Commission found: "almost all the District Collectors claimed that contractors were not engaged for MPLADS because guidelines prohibited that. However, the same is not corroborated by information gathered from the development functionaries and local people. Since many of the Government departments often do not have adequate infrastructure to implement the assigned works there is no other option than engaging private contractors for the purpose" (PEO, 2001: 75). The CAG performance appraisal No. 3A of 2001 pointed out that "in 23 test-checked constituencies in 10 states and UT, 1688 contracts were awarded by the DCs irregularly involving works costing Rs. 35.74 crore" (CAG, 2001: 15). In its 1998 report, the CAG had found in "182 cases valued Rs. 2.72 crores where the works were entrusted to the contractors, some of them sponsored by MPs...." (CAG, 1998: 74).

The stake of contractors and order suppliers in reaping profit and cultivating political patronage. M. Prakash describes the scheme as "cash cows", and wrote: "under this scheme, an MP can recommend projects in his constituency to administrative authorities for implementation through agencies of the state government. In practice, however, some MPs use the money to dole out contracts to agencies, who promise generous kickbacks in return". (Withering Development, Hardnews, October 2003). Even projects are selected by the contractors and suppliers using their political connections. "Evidence at the grassroots strongly indicates that local contractors and vested interests play the dominant role in identifying the projects" (Public Affairs Centre, Bangalore). P. Sainath depicted the situation in Andhra Pradesh: "If you are an elected representative you can guide many contractors towards yourself (or your wife). On the other hand, if you are a contractor, it makes sound sense to get yourself elected. Getting to be an MLA or MP also help you get permission to build, say, half a dozen engineering colleges" (The Hindu, ND).

All the stakes of the works contractors and order suppliers, as identified in the relative scales of (1) direct-indirect, (2) personal/individual-public/general perspectives and (3) relative intensity (Figure 3.8) is depicted below.

Words of Caution

The tabular and figurative framework used for analysing the different stakes of the eight principal stakeholders is based on ground-level information gathered from written material and interaction with hundreds of stakeholders. Under such circumstances; subjectivity in analysis cannot be avoided. And that is why we have taken measurement scales in relative terms. Thus, the conclusions that were drawn are indicative only in the sense that they only show the direction and dimension without quantifying them.

4
Line of Control Controversy (Federalism and Jurisdiction of the Wings of the State)

In 1999, newspapers in Kolkata, including a few national dailies, covered an MPLADS review meeting that was marked by pandemonium and drama. Ram Naik, the Minister of State in charge of MPLAD Scheme was in chair. Most MPs from West Bengal were present. The Trinamul Congress MPs were not happy with the execution of the MPLADS work and put the blame on the Calcutta Municipal Corporation (CMC) and the state government departments. On the other hand, the CMC and the state executing agencies were dissatisfied with the way the projects were recommended and the funds allocated. The MPs wanted to construct public toilets at their places of choice, that too with a budget of Rs. 50,000 each. The CMC wanted the public toilets to be constructed as per an approved design whose cost was much more than what the MPs offered. Secondly, the CMC had a plan of constructing and maintaining a number of public toilets for the whole city based on a survey. The location chosen by the MPs did not match CMC's plan, which resulted in a conflict. At a political level, West Bengal, ruled by the Left, is opposed to any move by the central government to interfere in its affairs. Citing federalism, the state government wanted only the funds for developmental schemes, but not the advice or directions of the central government. All these pose many a question on the limits of the MP Fund scheme as far as the nature of Indian federalism and decentralized planning is concerned.

MP Fund Scheme In Democratic Federalism

Union of States versus Federation of States

The history of Indian subcontinent has witnessed many forms of government - monarchy, federalism, republicanism and effective premiership. A few other forms of political formations were found in ample evidence. But the present constitution adopted a model of a "union of states" rather than a "federation of states". This is because of the Indian experience with a highly centralized colonial administration and an environment of pessimism during the days of independence as observed by Paul R. Brass, "India's constitution was born more in fear and trepidation than in hope and inspiration" (quoted from Saxena, 1999: 121). India's constitution-makers thought they had good reason to be fearful of disorder, even chaos, in the subcontinent as a consequence of the actions of a multiplicity of dangerous forces arising out of political movements associated with communalism, secessionism and revolutionary communism. The constitution of India was framed in response to the above-mentioned factors by a nationwide structure of one-party dominant system led by the Congress and a reasonably cohesive group of modernizing nationalist elites. In this context, Mahendra Prasad Singh observed: "India adopted in 1950 a heavily centralized system of parliamentary federalism under the dual impacts of the British colonial and nationalistic interventions" and "established an 'amicable union' combining parliamentary federal features" (Singh, 1995, chapter 8a:135). The federal features are highlighted briefly in subsequent paragraphs in order to place the role and functioning of the MP Fund scheme in proper perspective.

Territory Formation

Federalism, at its basic level, is concerned with formation of political and administrative spatial units within the national boundary. And, the Indian Constitution, in Article 3, confers unlimited powers on the Parliament to draw the territorial boundaries of the States and Union Territories and even change their names. This provision was used to rectify the colonial boundaries that were drawn arbitrarily and to make the spatial units consistent with cultural and ethnic boundaries. This provision was invoked in recent times to carve out three new states Jharkhand, Chattisgarh and Uttaranchal by splitting Bihar, Madhya Pradesh and Uttar Pradesh respectively.

Legislative Power

The Constitution lists three sets of subjects over which the legislative power of the Parliament and the State Assemblies are specified. They are the Union, State and Concurrent lists. Subjects of national relevance are included in the Union list, subjects of relevance to states are there in the State list and the Concurrent list contains subjects of mutual relevance. Residual powers are vested in the Parliament. However, the Union government is found to be more powerful, as the constitutional provision of law-making rests with the Parliament on all subjects, including the State list, under specific circumstances.

Administrative Jurisdictions

The constitution, under Article 256, ensures compliance of the state with the laws made by the Parliament and in the field of construction and maintenance of means of communication and transportation of national and military importance, and protection of railways. The Union government can proclaim emergency and impose President's Rule in a State under Article 356 when a situation arises in which a State cannot be governed according to the provisions of the Constitution. This 'safety valve, as devised by Dr. B.R. Ambedkar, is the most misused article that fulfills the political ambitions of the ruling parties in Delhi to dissolve the assemblies in opposition-ruled states. Even Governors plays a critical role in centre-state relations. Use of central services personnel for the administration of state secretariats, and central paramilitary forces (CRPF, BSF, CISF, etc.) for maintenance of law and order in the states are important administrative arrangements between the union and its states.

Financial Resource Sharing

The constitution provides specific instructions for mobilization and sharing of financial resources between the union and the states. Jurisdictions with regard to taxation and grant-in-aid are specified and for flexibility and adaptability, the President can periodically appoint a Finance Commission. Secondly the union government created a Planning Commission through an executive order to undertake economic and social development planning process and transfer of planed financial resources to the states. Though the state governments generally prefer devolution of fiscal resources though the Finance Commission, the role of Planning Commission gains ground due to the influence of the union government.

The center-state relations, as defined by the Constitution and as practised so far, are discussed in brief. But the process of federalization of Indian polities in the last half century has to be understood in order to appreciate and analyse a central intervention like the MP Fund scheme.

Federalism in a Dynamics Democracy

The Constitution says: "India, that is Bharat, shall be a Union of States". But Indian polity is a dynamic process that has to adapt to the center-state relationship under the parliamentary federal system. Seven factors, as identified by Mahendra Prasad Singh, are in play to influence the federalisation process in India. They are (1) the styles of Prime Ministerial leadership, (2) judicial and moral authority and structure, (3) the political party system, (4) the inter-regional and intra-regional disparities, (5) the ethnic identities, (6) class formation in the emerging structures of the mixed capitalist and state capitalist economy, and (7) the economic planning and centrally sponsored schemes of development. The last point is relevant for us. So, all other points, though important, would be discussed in brief.

Three models of premiership are identified to explain the federalisation dynamics of the Indian polity (Singh, 1995: 137). The "Parliamentary" model is ascribed to Jawaharlal Nehru, Lal Bahadur Shastri, and the early phase of Indira Gandhi (until the 1969 Congress split). The "Patrimonial" model is ascribed to the post 1969 premiership of Indira Gandhi. The "Federal" model is ascribed to the Janata phase (1977-79) and the National

Democratic Alliane (NDA) rule under Atal Bihari Vajpayee (1998-2004). The rest of the premiership, mainly that of Rajiv Gandhi and P.V. Narasimha Rao, followed a curious mixture of all the three models.

Center-state relations, a reflection of the federal dynamism, are shaped by the judicial and moral interventions while the Supreme Court gave judgments with regard to inter-state disputes and put forward advices in the matter of "question of law or fact" and of "public importance". It is now clear that the Parliament cannot alter the "basic structure" and the "essential features" of the Indian Constitution, federal division of powers being one such structure and feature. In recent years, it is observed that the role of judiciary is gaining ground to shape the federal nature of Indian Union due to changing nature of multi-party system of polarized pluralism, surfacing ethnic and societal diversity.

In order to understand the influence of political party system over the federalisation process, let us quote M.P. Singh: "To sum up, the trajectory of party system evaluation has passed through at least six stages: (1) Predominant Party System-I (1952-1969); (2) Multi Party System-I (1969-1971); (3) Predominant Party System-II (1971-1977); (4) Two Party System (1977-1984); (5) (a stillborn) Predominant Party System-III (1984-1989); and (6) Multi Party System-II (1989- to date). The transition from one party dominance to a more competitive, pluralist party system has been a factor contributing to the greater federalisation of India's predominantly parliamentary system"(Singh, 1995:142). He also observed, "with the Party system becoming one of a multipartisan polarized pluralism in 1989, and then again in 1991, parliamentary power not only in the Rajya Sabha but also in the Lok Sabha has become more maneuverable to the federal forces in the polity."

Federalism may be considered as an institutional arrangement to solve intra-societal (ethnic, class and linguistic identities) conflicts and tensions in a plural and diversified society. This is true of the Indian case as well. The anti-colonial discourse of India's struggle for independence from self-assertion and dominance of advanced nationalists, shaped the Indian federal structure in the post-independence period. Creation of states based on linguistic and ethnic identities resulted in creation of Tamil Nadu, Andhra Pradesh, Punjab, Haryana, Himachal Pradesh, Goa and the seven sister states of North East. Federalism, as influenced by ethnic forces, is the most visible in cases of constitution of Autonomous District Councils in Assam, Meghalaya and Mizoram as Sixth Schedule areas. Article 371 of the constitution has special provisions for the States of Maharashtra and Gujarat (development boards, etc.) and Article 371A with respect to the State of Nagaland (religion/social practices, customary law, ownership and transfer of land, etc.). Though different, such special provisions are made for seven more states - Assam, Manipur, Andhra Pradesh, Sikkim, Mizoram, Arunachal Pradesh and Goa - under part-XXI of the Constitution. But the most talked about and sentimentally charged is Article 370, which grants autonomy to Jammu & Kashmir. Lastly, the discussion on federalization process is incomplete if we do not mention the recent developments that resulted in creation of Darjeeling Autonomous Hill Council in West Bengal and the Bodoland Autonomous Council in Assam.

Money Sharing - the Game of Indian Federalism

Economic well-being is the aspiration of every society. Lots of financial resource is required to meet the societal demand for basic needs like health, education, social security and employment. More funds are required for building infrastructure like roads, railways, airways, telecommunication and research and development facilities. Further, additional funds are required to achieve a higher rate of economic growth that demands higher rate of capital formation for investment in irrigation projects, heavy industries, and technological upgradation of various sectors. Thus, availability of funds is the main constraint, and overcoming that, is the prime objective of the government. The state and local governments in India are perpetually in deficit to meet the demands for both welfare and economic activities. So they compete with each other to mobilize more financial resources. When the internal resource mobilization capacity of the states is limited, it is obvious for them to rely more on the central government. Three institutional mechanisms transfer funds from the resource rich union government to the states and UTs. They are: (i) the Finance Commission awards, (ii) Planning Commission grants and loans, and (iii) the central schemes. In a federal democracy, the states clamor for more and more plan resource grants of the Planning Commission, and also for higher awards from the Finance Commission. The federal process can be understood by watching the negotiating skills of the state governments while sharing the financial cake amongst themselves and with the union government.

Finance Commission Awards

In pursuance of the provisions of Article 280 of the Constitution and of the Finance Commission (Miscellaneous Provisions) Act, 1951, the President constitutes a Finance Commission (FC) mainly to distribute the net proceeds of shareable taxes between the centre and the states and also to allocate funds to the States. Till date, 12 such commissions have been set up. The objectives of FCs can be understood if we take note of the observation made by the 11th FC set up for the period 2000-2005:

> A sound system of inter-governmental fiscal transfers constitutes the cornerstone of a strong and stable federal polity. Transfers serve a two-fold purpose: one, to address the vertical imbalance – the inadequacy of revenues of sub-national governments to meet their expenditure liabilities, arising from asymmetrical assignment of functional responsibilities and financial powers among different governmental levels, and two, to alleviate horizontal imbalances, the disparities in the revenue capacity of the constituent units of the federation – the states and local bodies in our case – in order that all of them may be in a position to provide basic public services to their citizens at a reasonable level (Report of the Eleventh Finance Commission, 2000: 6).

A study of the method followed by all these FCs and the role played by the stakeholder states gives ample evidence of the federalization dynamics in India. States with cities like Kolkata, Mumbai, Chennai and Delhi demand higher share as they feel taxes are mostly collected in these financial centers.

Populous states like Uttar Pradesh, Bihar and West Bengal demand higher weights to population. Poor states like Orissa, Bihar, Madhya Pradesh, Assam and North eastern States request for more funds from FCs to meet higher developmental demands. States having lower tax base pleaded for higher share to bridge the gaps in their revenue accounts. The arrangements and petitions of the State Governments are accommodated by the FCs by following some sort of normative procedures. Rupees 3,76,318 crore were proposed to be transferred during 2000-2005 to all the States from the share in central taxes and duties as per the 11th FCs recommendations on a normative basis.

Table 4.1
Inter se Sharing of Union Taxes

Sl. No.	Criteria	Relative weight (percentage)		
		10th FC	11th FC	12th FC
1.	Population	20.0	10.0	25.0
2.	Income (Distance Method)	60.0	62.5	50.0
3.	Area	5.0	7.5	10.0
4.	Index of Infrastructure	5.0	7.5	-
5.	Tax Effort	10.0	5.0	7.5
6.	Fiscal Discipline	-	7.5	7.5
	Total	100.0	100.0	100.0

For meeting the requirements of states for upgradation of standards in non-developmental and social sectors and services, particularly of States which are backward in general administration, with a view to modernize and rationalize the administrative set up in the interest of speed, efficiency and sound fiscal management, the 11th FC allotted Rs. 40332 crore to States. The 11th FC, following the footprints of the earlier FCs, recommended Rs. 8,255 crore for meeting the relief expenditure of the natural and other calamities. Lastly, the local panchayats and municipalities got Rs. 10,000 crore between 2000 and 2005 from the Commission to supplement their resource base. Distribution among the states followed the criteria and weights of population (40 per cent), index of decentralization (20 percent), distance from the highest per capital income (20 per cent), revenue effort (10 percent) and geographical area (10 per cent). Total transfer to the states, as recommended by the 11th FC for the period 2002-2005, stands at Rs. 4,34,905 crore.

Development Planning and Central Schemes

Before independence, India was a poor and underdeveloped country. All economic sectors used low-end technology resulting in low productivity. At the top of this, there were widespread regional disparities in economic and social welfare indices. To achieve economic development at a faster rate and bridge the gap between the rich and the poor states, "five-year plans" were adopted. "In India, we have opted for a five year medium-term plan, anchored in a rolling perspective, plan normally of 15 years, as an instrument for bringing about planned socio-economic development. A five-year plan is an indicative plan of action over ensuing five years reflecting largely the intent of the Government for that period at the national, regional and the sectional level. The provisioning of the indicated plan outlay and the annual break-up of physical targets in respect of various programmes and schemes, if any, are operationalised through allocations made in each of the annual plans constituting that period". (Planning Commission, 2002: 27). As the planning exercise is all about financial resource allocation, within a framework and its correlation with economic factors like physical resources, technology and welfare interstate and intrastate allocation becomes prime concern for the planners. In a federal democracy, the states clamor for more and more plan resources.

The method followed by the Planning Commission to allocate funds to states differs from that of the FCs. While the latter work out the transfer based on normative methods to strengthen the equalizing role of fiscal transfer (Bagchi, 2000: 121), the former allots funds to all states/UTs based on the requirements that arise after calculation of the macro-economic and sectoral economic parameters like growth rates of gross domestic product and employment, trade and balance of payment gaps, capital, out-put ratios and sectoral allocation, and the internal resource mobilizing capabilities of the individual states. K.C. Pant, the former Deputy Chairman of the Planning Commission wrote in the preface to the 10th Five Year Plan (2002-2007) document: "The potentials and constraints that exist at the state-level vary significantly. Therefore, for the first time, we have broken down the national targets to the states level in consultation with State Governments.... This will enable the states to better focus their own developmental plans by more careful consideration of the sectoral pattern of growth and its regional dispersion within the states". The union government's powerful hand to implement the centralized planning process of India is more explicit in the words of the Deputy Chairman, "The Planning Commission is preparing a series of State Development Reports, which will take stock of the capabilities of each state and develop appropriate strategies" (10th Five Year Plan Document, Vol.1, preface).

The union government implements hundreds of developmental and welfare schemes. All those schemes that are funded fully by the union government but executed by the state agencies are called central sector schemes. All other schemes that are funded by both the union and state governments as partners, but executed by the state agencies are called centrally-sponsored schemes. Most of the activities covered by these

Table 4.2
Resource Transfer to States and Union Territories by the Union Government

	Transfer Items	Year 1981-82	Year 1991-92	Year 2001-02
1	States' share of taxes and duties	5328	17199	52845
		(56.71)	(40.57)	(50.01)
2	Non-plan grants & loans	1235	3244	17276
		(13.15)	(7.65)	(16.35)
	Finance Commission awards (1+2)	6563	20443	70121
		(69.86)	(48.22)	(66.36)
3	Central assistance for states and UT Plans	3168	13732	36077
		(33.72)	(32.39)	(34.14)
4	Assistance for central and centrally sponsored schemes	1032	5888	9875
		(10.98)	(13.89)	(9.35)
5	Less recovery of loans and advances	1368	3167	10412
		(14.56)	(7.47)	(9.85)
6	Net resource transfer	9395	42396	105661
		(100.00)	(100.00)	(100.00)

Note: Figures in parenthesis is percentage to net resource transfer. The amounts are revised estimates.

Source: various union government budgets.

schemes are in fact assigned to the state governments by the Constitution of India. The following list highlights how the union government is into activities that are not only outside its jurisdiction, but also are insignificant and inconsequential in nature. However, the union government transfers more than 10 percent of its net resource transfer to states and UTs through these schemes (Table 4.2).

The state governments have, from time to time, in the National Development Council (NDC), of which all the Chief Ministers are members, objected to the ways in which the union government schemes are imposed on them. The resource crunch at the state level comes in the way of the execution of centrally-sponsored schemes. They also doubt the rational of these schemes that are designed at the centre. So the 43rd NDC (December 1991) decided to transfer 113 such schemes to the states/UTs. In practice, even after a decade, only a few hand-picked schemes are transferred to the States or are modified a little. For example, "assistance to the states were given for implementing programmes as per scale/contents determined by the Government of India. To provide freedom and flexibility to the State Governments, for implementations of various centrally-sponsored schemes on MOU basis, the new scheme 'Supplementation/complementation on State's efforts through work plans (Macro Management)' has been formulated by integrating 28 ongoing schemes" operational from 2000-01 by the Ministry of Agriculture (Government of India, Expenditure Budget 2000-2001, Vol. 2: 9). On the other hand, the states are pressuring the union government to convert all these schemes to either fully-funded central sector schemes or transfer the complete funds as grant-in-aid. This is federal polity at its most vibrating dynamics and it gets its energy from the ruling party compositions of different states/UTs on the one hand and at the union government level on the other.

FEDERAL POLITY AND MP FUND SCHEME

The rationale for a full centrally-sponsored scheme like MP Fund can be seen in our federal polity in the context that was explained above. Apart from being a substantial amount, the

Rs. 1580 crore spent under this scheme every year constitutes a large share of the resource transfer to the states and UTs under central and centrally-sponsored schemes. That means, the state, district and local governments loose the constitutional powers that were vested upon them in so far as the allocation of subjects goes. Incidentally, all the 23 items under the MPLAD scheme are from 29 items mentioned in 11th Schedule of the Constitution. "This scheme is entirely against the letter and spirit of the Constitution (73rd Amendment) Act". (*The Hindu*, Online edition, 3 Feb., 2001).

MP Fund in Panchayati Raj Framework

Though the provisions contained in the Directive Principles of State Policy are not enforceable by the court of law, the Constitution clarifies in the Article 37 that "the principles therein laid down are nevertheless fundamental in the governance of the country". And, one of the main directives is that "the state shall take steps to organise village panchayats and endow them with such powers and authority as may be necessary to enable them to function as units of self government". Accordingly, the 73rd and 76th constitutional Amendments were made to set up and empower village panchayats (local self-governing bodies). The *gram* (village) and *nagar* (town) panchayats have the power and responsibility to prepare plans for and implement schemes for economic development and social justice as may be entrusted to them including those in relation to 29 subjects listed in the Eleventh Schedule (Article 243 G) in case of *gram* panchayats and in relation to 18 subjects listed in the Twelfth Schedule (Article 243 W of the Constitution) in case of *nagar* panchayats and municipal councils and corporations. The works that are allowed under the MP Fund scheme are also reserved for the *gram* and *nagar* panchayats. Both want to develop their constituencies and the public welfare. Both approach the public periodically and beg for votes. But the ways and means at their disposal differs perceptibly. This conflict of interest is as natural as the downward movement of water.

The stories of conflict of interest between the MPs and the members of Panchayats have been recorded by the press from time to time. Even the Public Action Center in Bangalore thinks that the "funds meant for local development are made available to MPs totally outside the domain of the panchayats. It was also agreed that funds for the scheme were siphoned off from rural development allocation, which following the 73rd Amendment, should have gone to panchayats". The conflict becomes acute when the *gram* panchayat and *nagar* panchayat bodies are dominated by a party to which the MPs do not belong. For example, the "Trinmool Congress leader, Ms. Mamta Banerjee has strongly criticized the move by the Calcutta Municipal Corporation to ask the principal of the Tiljala Brajanath Vidyapith in the city to consult the local MLA or Ward Councilor about the funds for renovating the school. The fund is part of the money from the MPLADS allocated to Ms. Mamta Banerjee. She has decided to take the issue in the Lok Sabha and call for a privilege motion" (Calcutta Online, 29 March, 1999).

Both the MPs and the Panchayat Raj Institution (PRI) *panchs* (representatives) are people's representatives at different levels. The conflict is in their legislative roles But when the question of making financial resource available and execution of developmental works comes into play, conflict of interest arises. Jurisdictional questions come to the forefront, too. A way to capture this sphere of conflict is to measure the financial muscle of the MPs vis-à-vis the *panchs*. But the task is very difficult. We know the financial strength of the MPs (Rs. 2 crore per year), but not that of the *panchs*. This is because, as the Eleventh Finance Commission noticed, "the schemes related to the subjects included in the Eleventh and Twelfth Schedules have not yet been transferred to these bodies (PRIs) in most of the states. States' legislation merely enumerate the subjects indicated in the two schedules but do not specify the schemes that have to be implemented by these bodies as contemplated in article 243 G and 243 W." Secondly, the role of *panchs* in utilizing large sums allotted for rural and urban development through the central sector or centrally-sponsored schemes (CSS) is also confusing. The Eleventh FC observed, "in some cases, the local bodies have been associated but they are merely performing agency functions with no decisive role clearly assigned to them in the preparation and implementation of the schemes" (Report of the Eleventh Finance Commission, 2000: 83).

Since the options are limited, we can rely on some approximations. The hundred odd list of CSS were scanned to identify the best few to measure the financial strength of the *panchs*. First we zero in on all schemes that have resulted in creation of physical assets to meet local needs. Secondly, we have listed within them a few schemes that give opportunities to the *panchs* to exercise power, and to choose and implement the projects. The most apt scheme is the Sampoorna Grameen Rozgar Yojana (SGRY), funded by the Ministry of Rural Development and effective since April 2002. The secondary objective of SGRY is to create durable community, social and economic assets and develop infrastructure in rural areas. Funds and food grains under this scheme are earmarked for zilla parishad, Intermediate panchayats and Village panchayats in a particular formula. In some cases, the PRI members distribute the available funds among themselves and execute the projects. Table 4.3 gives the comparative strength of PRIs and the MPs in terms of resource availability. In all the states, the *panchs* have much more resource at their disposal than the MPs. If we add all the CSS that empower the *panchs* financially, then it becomes clear that the MPs' power is no match to the power of the *panchs*.

MP Fund in the State Governance Business Framework

There are 30 states and 5 union territories in India. They have 3971 members of legislative assemblies (MLAs/*Vidhayaks*). The Constitution, in Article 246, in List-II in the Seventh Schedule enumerated 66 subject matters on which the state legislatures have exclusive powers to make laws for their states or any part thereof. The states spend thousands of crores on the development and welfare of citizens. The *Vidhayaks* enjoy exclusive MLA funds and can execute many works of local nature. In this environment, one has to examine the role played by the MP fund within the federal polity. Let us try to approach this subject from two angles. First, the financial strength of MPs vis-a-vis the MLAs due to the respective schemes. Second, analysis of the roles and the attitudes of the state governments towards the execution of MP Fund projects.

Table 4.3
Funds and Food grains availability under SGRY and MPLAD Schemes for Community Assets Creation, 2002-2003

States	*SGRY Funds and Food available*		*MPLADS*
	Funds (Rs. in crore)	*Food grains (in tonnes)*	*Funds available (Rs. in crore)*
1	2	3	4
Andhra Pradesh	308.2	210925	120
Arunachal Pradesh	15.6	12294	6
Assam	391.3	319224	42
Bihar	516.5	401384	112
Chattishgarh	154.9	101188	32
Goa	1.10	1921	6
Gujarat	97.6	86724	74
Haryana	71.0	47805	30
Himachal Pradesh	36.4	20131	14
Jammu & Kashmir	37.9	23898	20
Jharkhand	356.3	276903	40
Karnataka	240.8	156355	80
Kerala	97.9	70159	58
Madhya Pradesh	342.2	244231	80
Maharastra	415.8	310772	134
Manipur	12.2	21413	6
Meghalaya	26.4	23996	6
Mizoram	8.7	5553	4
Nagaland	8.3	16460	4
Orissa	325.7	236818	62
Punjab	48.5	40481	40
Rajasthan	207.5	118840	70
Sikkim	6.5	6150	4
Tamil Nadu	256.5	183793	114
Tripura	46.2	38668	6
Uttaranchal	67.5	47303	16
Uttar Pradesh	1143.5	701653	222
West Bengal	420.1	263182	116
Andaman & Nicober Islands	0.4	1611	2
Dadra & Nagar Haveli	0.6	1228	2
Daman & Diu	0.0	375	2
Lakhadweep	0.2	593	2
Pondicherry	2.3	1603	4
Total	**5664.6**	**3993750**	**1530**

Note: Funds and food grains available is calculated by putting aside 22.5% of funds/food-grains earmarked for individual beneficiaries allocated to zilla and intermediate panchayats as stipulated under the SGRY scheme.

Source: Ministry of Rural Development, Annual Report 2003-2004

Comparison between the MP Fund scheme and the MLA Fund scheme is more appropriate in the democratic, vote-capturing framework than the federal administrative jurisdiction framework. The outcome depends on the relationship between an MP and the MLAs in a particular constituency. The relationships are dynamic, flexible and mostly deceptive. Under the democratic vote-capturing framework, they might either be in cooperative or in conflicting mode. One can compare their financial power in terms of the discretionary funds they have at their disposal that influences the voters (refer annexure: 1.2 of chapter 1)

In most of the states, the MLAs have more discretionary funds at their disposal than those of the MPs. This is despite the fact that many states are in a financial crunch. The MLAs of Andhra, Assam, rajasthan and Maharashtra having more money in their hand are more equipped to meet the local needs than the MPs. At times, this has resulted in conflict of ego and interest. One of the main reasons of introducing the Fund scheme was to empower the MPs financially. But over the years, parity between them in terms of financial resources could not be maintained. Politicians apply different strategies- mostly disguised- to counter their rivals, the ultimate aim being to capture power. Parsuram Majhi, 13th Lok Sabha, MP from Navrangpur in Orissa revealed: "four MLAs are competing with me in a single village and the nearby localities with the help of MLA funds". The relationships and the moves adopted by both the MPs and MLAs in a democratic vote-capturing framework is depicted in pictorial models in Figure 4.1.

A single MP and a numbers of MLAs represent a parliamentary constituency. The situation differs from state to state. The number of MLAs per MP is as high as 30 in Tripura and 20 in case of Arunachal Pradesh. On the other hand, it is only four in Chattishgarh and five in Uttaranchal and Uttar Pradesh combined. The MP and the MLAs may be from the same political party or alliance, or from different political

Figure 4.1

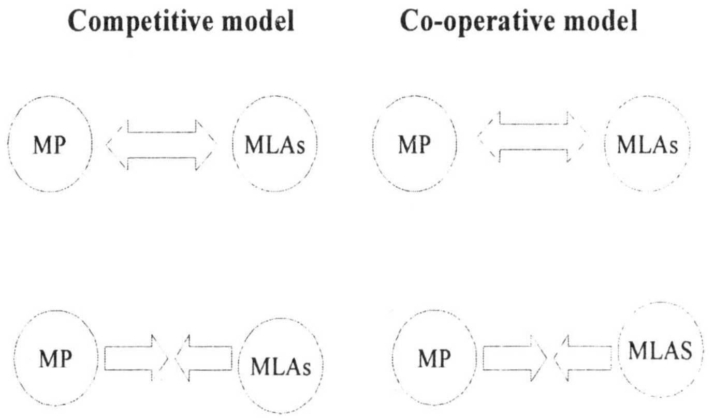

affiliations. The nature of politics determines their relationships. They may cooperate with each other or maybe in conflicting or competitive mode.

The state governments perceive the Lok Sabha MPs as the agents of the central government. This perception becomes more distinct when the political party of the MP is different from the ruling party in the state. As the MP Fund scheme projects are invariably executed by state agencies, the nature of the relationship between the MPs and the state government determines the pace of the execution. Funds released by the centre go to the district collector or magistrate, who has the power to offload the projects to the executing agencies. Since he works for the state government- mostly for the chief ministers- and is only accountable to the state government, his performance is subject to the directions and the stands of the state government. Thus the success of the MP Fund scheme depends largely on the mood of the state government. "One official says the scheme has flopped because the government did not take into account the fact that, for an MP, his constituency means potential voters and not the community per se. There is political rivalry between the MPs and opposition-ruled state government. The latter often asks district collectors to prevent the former form carrying out developmental projects" (The Rediff Special, 18 Dec., 2000).

Hypothesis

The MPLADS funds utilisation would be better for those MPs whose party is also in power in the state.

The utilisation of the MP Fund during the 13th Lok Sabha period can be analysed to prove this point. Let us keep in mind

Table 4.4
Ruling Political Parties of the State Governments and the Lok Sabha MPs in 13th Lok Sabha Period (October 1999 to May 2004)

Sl. No	*States*	*Party in power in state government* — *Most of the period & Rest of the period*			*No. of MPs (LS)*	*Percentage of funds sanctioned to that release d by GoI*	*Percentage of expenditure to sanctioned funds*
1	2	3	4	5	6	7	8
1	Andhra Pradesh	TDP (NDA)		Ruling	36	103.1	89.16
				Opposition	6	99.53	82.82
2	Assam	INC		Ruling	11	99.60	93.55
				Opposition	3	104.72	89.60
3	Bihar	RJD		Ruling	5	96.12	88.59
				Opposition	35	99.14	88.24
4	Chattishgah	INC	BJP	Ruling	3	99.69	100.07
				Opposition	8	97.15	91.96
5	Gujarat	BJP		Ruling	21	99.47	90.87
				Opposition	5	100.51	86.72
6	Jharkhand	BJP (NDA)		Ruling	10	98.72	82.20
				Opposition	11	89.85	80.89
7	Karnataka	INC		Ruling	19	104.83	93.26
				Opposition	9	107.75	96.99
8	Kerala	INC (UDF)		Ruling	10	105.10	80.58
				Opposition	9	101.14	78.26
9	Madhya Pradesh	INC	BJP	Ruling	7	104.37	86.47
				Opposition	22	100.43	93.73
10	Maharashtra	INC plus NCP		Ruling	15	104.51	87.27
				Opposition	33	103.01	82.73
11	Orissa	BJD plus BJP		Ruling	19	98.61	81.27
				Opposition	2	96.63	96.52
12	Punjab	SAD	INC	Ruling	3	98.90	70.99
				Opposition	9	101.98	84.43
13	Rajasthan	INC	BJP	Ruling	10	107.53	93.52
				Opposition	15	102.96	95.48
14	Tamil Nadu	AIDMK	DMK	Ruling	11	101.65	101.05
				Opposition	28	101.00	95.36
15	Uttar Pradesh	NDA/ NDF	SP	Ruling	42	97.52	89.27
				Opposition	38	98.52	91.13
16	Uttaranchal	BJP	INC	Ruling	4	98.63	96.72
				Opposition	1	102.91	90.30
17	West Bengal	LF		Ruling	29	98.63	69.36
				Opposition	13	103.33	77.26

Note: Small states and UTs have not been considered as they have very few MPs in the Lok Sabha. Haryana, Himachal Pradesh, Jammu & Kashmir and Delhi are not considered as the MPs of these states are predominantly from one party.

that multiple factors determine MP Fund utilisation. However, the relationship between the MP and the state government is probably the most influential one.

Though the results are mixed, Table 4.4 findings mostly support our hypothesis. Findings in ten out of 17 states show that, the funds utilisation (column 8) is relatively less in case of opposition party MPs in comparison to the MPs of the ruling party of the state. These states are Andhra Pradesh, Assam, Bihar, Chattishgarh, Gujarat, Jharkhand, Kerala, Maharashtra, Tamil Nadu and Uttaranchal. On the other hand, the utilisation position is relatively better for the MPs of the opposition parties in seven states of Karnataka, Madhya Pradesh, Orissa, Punjab, Rajasthan, Uttar Pradesh and West Bengal. In a federal polity, the MP Fund scheme is reluctantly executed by the state and district administrations. This reluctant environment prevails due to conflict of interest amongst the political parties and between the bureaucrats and the legislature.

The attack on the line of control between the federal domains along with their complexities is addressed in the above sections. However, we would like to conclude this exploration by drawing attention to the thesis advocated by Pran Chopra while analysing the 2003 assembly election results in Madhya Pradesh. He believes that, "this outcome is a vote for more federalism". The panchayats saw the harm being done to the Panchayati raj system in the name of reforming it by chief minister Digvijay Singh by introducing the concept of "district governments". "Just as they (MLAs) themselves used the dynamics of democratic federalism to dilute the powers of MPs at the union-state level of federalism, panchayat leaders can use the same dynamics against them at the level of sub-state federalism...Now it appears that panchayat leaders in Madhya Pradesh have used their electoral clout to press for their priorities...They now believe that power to influence elections has become indispensably a tool in sub-State federalism as MLAs themselves have found it to be in union-state federalism." (Pran Chopra, A Vote for Federalism, *The Hindu*,ND, 9 Jan., 2004)

MP FUND SCHEME AND WINGS OF THE STATE

Legislative, executive and judiciary are the three wings of the state. Those who framed the Indian Constitution were aware of the political philosophy propagated by western thinkers like Socrates, Plato, Aristotle, John Locke and John Stuart Mill. They also observed the functioning of the government in different countries and the role played by their constitutions in shaping the domain of its three wings. Though loose, the Indian Constitution has defined the respective jurisdictions of the legislative (part V, chapter-II and part VI, chapter III), executive (part V, chapter I and part VI, chapter II) and judiciary (part V, chapter IV and part VI, chapter V). The half-a-century history of the working of the Indian constitution would reveal that, the wings of state are in agreement on their jurisdictional boundaries-*a la* the line of control.

The Legislative

The legislative business is the responsibility of the parliament and the state assemblies. The subjects on which they can make laws are listed in the seventh schedule as union list (97 items), state list (66 items) and concurrent list (47 items). Bills are introduced and passed in the parliament and the assemblies. MLAs and MPs have the power to pass a bill and make a law. But many parliamentarians take minimum interest in legislative work. Either they are busy in some other work, leaving very little time to attend to the duties for which they are elected, or they deliberately neglect the legislative business for political and individual gains.

Sharad Gupta observed: "For parliamentarians preoccupied with alternative professions or those behind bars, attending house sessions is a obligation better left unfulfilled." (Missing in Action, *India Today*, March 4, 2002). On a few illustrious MPs, he wrote:

> Filmstar Raj Babbar was in Ladakh late last year, shooting for J. P. Gupta's film *LoC*, with another three films on the floor. Charting the careers of his children Aryan and Juhi, who are making their film debut, is also a matter of

priority. Which, of course, leaves little time for sundry errands. Like attending the Lok Sabha, where he represents the important Agra constituency. Babbar attended the Lok Sabha for only five days during the 2001 winter session.

It's over two years now that the President nominated Lata Mangeshkar to the Rajya Sabha. She did come for the swearing in ceremony. But Parliament has seen next to nothing of her since. India's nightingale has either been absent or on leave since.

Sarad Power (Lok Sabha), party: NCP, State: Maharashtra, attended 2001 winter session for 12 days. Sakshi Maharaj (Rajya Sabha), party: Samajbadi Party, State: Uttar Pradesh, could not attend the house even for a single day. Same is the case with Ashok Chandel (LS), D. N. Rao (RS). Shahabuddin (LS), K. Karunakaran (LS), Ambareesh (LS), S. S. Vaghela (LS) and A. B. A Ghani Khan Chaudhury (LS) who attended the house for 7 days, 2 days, 7 days, 12 days and 12 days respectively.

Not attending the parliamentary sessions and to the legislative business by design has become common in recent times. At the slightest pretext, the parliamentarians either create pandemonium or boycott proceedings. Let us analyse their attendance:

Figure 4.2

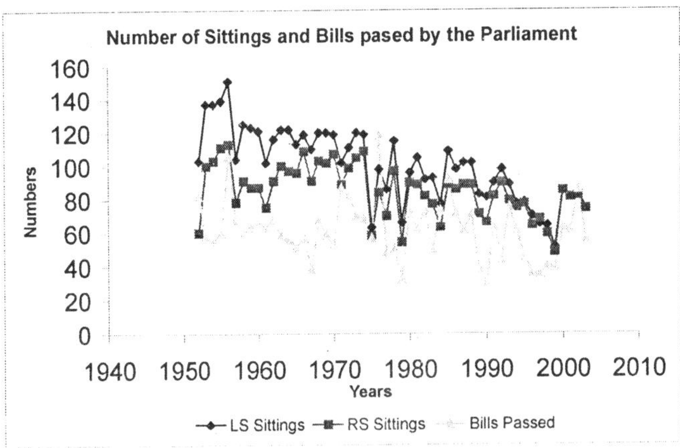

The negligence by the MPs to perform legislative business reached a pick when the Finance Bill, Demand for the Grants for the Railways as well as the Union Budget were passed without debate in the Budget session of 2004. The acrimony between the ruling United Progressive Alliance (UPA) government and opposition National Democratic Alliance (NDA) led to premature end of the budget session resulting in loss of 47 hours of precious time of the Lok Sabha. Speaker Somnath Chatterjee, commented, "It is destructive of the basic tenets of parliamentary functioning when disrespect is deliberately shown to the Chair. Some members seek to behave as super-speaker. Who will speak, when he will speak, what subject will be discussed and how the business will be conducted now seem to be decided on the floor and the Chair seems to have no role to play" (Purnima S. Tripathi, Democratic Dysfunction, *Frontline*, Vol. 21 (19), 2004). Even the Prime Minister Dr. Manmohan Singh lamented that "never in the history of any goveronment, the first 100 days have been characterized by the daily turmoil that we witness in Parliament", and added, "I had to deal with many of these abnormal situations" (*Times of India*, ND, 25 Aug., 2004).

The Judiciary

Judicial business is the responsibility of the Supreme Court of India, the High Courts in the states, special courts and the other courts at sub-state level. The Supreme Court has original jurisdiction (federal disputes: Article 131), appellate jurisdiction in civil and criminal matters (Article 133 and 134) and in many other areas. Similarly, the High Courts and other courts have to perform the judicial business within the prescribed boundaries.

These days the judiciary is becoming more pro-active to perform duties that are the responsibility of the executive and the legislature. Judicial activism in the field of legislative business, which is the prime responsibility of the Parliament and the Sate Legislative Assemblies, is based on the radical judgments rendered by the Court by discovering the "basic features" of the constitution and by introduction of the "due process clause" in its substantive and procedural aspects in the reading of the Article 21 and 14 and generation of numerous rights and freedoms not explicitly given in Part III of the

Constitution. The Court assumes the legislative role "where gaps and ambiguities exist in the law or where the full protection of Fundamental Rights warranted enunciation of a new policy or extension of an exiting policy in conformity with the constitutional scheme and international obligations of the State" (N. R. Madhava Menon, Parliament and the Judiciary, *The Hindu*, ND, 26 Sept., 2004:16).

The basic features of the Constitution

The Supreme Court overruled the decision in the *Golaknath case* (fundamental rights cannot be abrogated even by an amendment of the Constitution because amendments are also laws within the meaning of Article 13) by a majority of 7 to 6 in the *Keshavananda Bharati Case*, and declared that the Constitution has certain "basic features' that cannot be altered or destroyed at all through the amendment process.

The due process clause

The Supreme Court while interpreting equality before law (Article 14), observed that all Articles on Fundamental Rights bear a relationship with one another and any law depriving a person of any of the liberties or freedom must not only satisfy the requirements of Article 21 (procedure established by law) but also article 19 (equality before the law). Based on the principle of 'reasonableness', the Court introduced the 'due process clause' in place of the 'procedure established by law' provision advocated by Article 21. "By re-interpreting Article 14, 19 and 21 and by refusing to take note of the rejection of the 'due process clause' in the Constituent Assembly, the judges have given to themselves the unchallengeable authority to strike down any legislation or other state action solely not appear to them to be 'reasonable, just and fair'. " (N. R. Madhava Menon, Parliament and the Judiciary, *The Hindu*, ND, 26 Sept., 2004: 16).

The Judiciary is found to be proactive in executive functions while it observes that the laws are left unimplemented and the individual rights or public interest are adversely affected thereby. A few of the judgments to execute welfare and developmental projects are listed:

Anganwadi: "The Supreme Court today [29 April, 2004] directed the Centre and the States to make operational by the end of August all *Anganwadi* centers run under the Integrated Child Development Scheme for the benefit of children and mother.... It directed the Government to provide nutritional food to all children in the zero-to-six year category who attend the *Anganwadis*" (*The Hindu*, ND, 30 April, 2004: 17).

Industries in Delhi's Residential Areas

"A Bench of justice Y. K. Sabharwal and justice B. N. Agrawal passing orders (7 May, 2004) on a petition filed by M. C. Mehta fixed a time-frame for different categories of industries for stoppage of their operations, ranging from four months to 18 months...referring to the affidavit field by the Delhi government in the Court, the Bench said there were 1.26 lakhs industrial units functioning in Delhi, of which 1.01 lakhs were in residential/non-conforming areas and only 25,000 in approved industrial area. It was stated that shifting 1.01 lakh units illegally operating in residential areas would result in hardship to approximately seven lakh families...Rejecting the contention, the Bench said there was no justification for the Government to take on such a stand for violation of law and throwing to the wind the norms of environment, public health and safety (*The Hindu*, 8 May, 2004: 1).

Seat reservation in medical and engineering college

The Supreme Court extended for 2004-05 its 1994 order directing the Tamil Nadu Government to create extra seats in medical, engineering and other courses to accommodate meritorious students in the 'Open category' who had been affected by the 69 per cent reservation policy. As per the 1994 order, the number of seats so created would be equal to the number of seats the 'Open category' candidates would have got had the rule of 50 per cent reservation been applied, instead of 69 per cent.

National anthem recital compulsory

The Patna High Court made the recital of National anthem in all primary and secondary schools compulsory in Bihar (*The Hindu*, 31 Aug., 2004, New Delhi).

Tiny Tots case

"The Delhi High Court today [31 August 2004] sought assistance of the Attorney-General of India, Milon Banerjee and people in general to decide an appeal seeking a ban on interviewing children and their parents for admission to nursery and pre-primary classes..." (*The Hindu*, 1 Sept., 2004, New Delhi).

Medical College Admission

"The Supreme Court today (1 September, 2004) directed the Director General of Health Services (DGHS) to conduct another round of counseling to fill the 122 vacant seats in MBBS course (of the total 1550 seats) and 38 seats under BDS course (out of 144 seats) under 15 percent quota in government medical colleges...A three-judge bench...directed the DGHS to complete the counseling by September 8 and gave the students time till September 13 to join the course" (*The Hindu*, ND, 2 September, 2004).

Adult movies and programmes on TV

"The Bombay High Court restricted nine satellite TV channels from beaming adult movies or programmes without the prior permission of the Central Board of Film Certification... The order came on a public interest litigation (PIL) filed by a teacher of St. Xavier College...(*The Hindu*, ND, 2 Sep., 2004).

Ban on manual scavenging

"The Court [Supreme Court] issued notice in January [2004] to the centre, all states and union territories on a petition seeking firm action for eradication of the degrading practice of 'manual scavenging' in which over 12 lakh persons are engaged across the country and implement a scheme for their proper rehabilitation" (*The Hindu*, ND, 14 Sept., 2004).

Chief Justice of India (CJI) V. N. Khare's order scuttled the government's move to appoint a bureaucrat as the head of the Competition Commission. That judgment disapproved of the trend of the Executive to usurp judicial functions by appointing civil servants as head of tribunals. In an interview to *The Hindu*, he said, "it is not our intention or desire to ask the Executive to do this or do that. Only when the Executive fails to perform its statutory obligations, the necessity for us to interfere arises" (*The Hindu*, ND, 2 May, 2004: 8). But the former CJI, A. S. Anand while defending the judicial activism cautioned to ensure that the activism does not become "judicial adventurism". He opined, "Judicial whistle needs to be blown for a purpose and with caution. It is to be remembered that Court cannot run the Government. The Court have the duty of implementing the constitutional safeguards that protect individual rights but they cannot push back the limits of the Constitution to accommodate the challenged violation" (*The Hindu*, ND, 26 Sept., 2004: 16).

The Executive

The Parliamentary political system was chosen by the makers of Indian constitution to establish a strong executive in the context of the political and social situation that arose due to partition, formation and integration of states. Subsequently, the Executive wing was designed to meet the challenges of developing the country that was predominantly agrarian, underdeveloped and unequal. "On the eve of the departure of the British, on 14 August 1947, Jawaharlal Nehru declared: 'Long years ago we made a tryst with destiny, and now the time comes when we shall redeem our pledge.' 'The achievement we celebrate today,' Nehru went on, 'is but a step, an opening of opportunity, to the great triumphs and achievements that await us.' He reminded the country that the task ahead included 'the ending of poverty and ignorance and disease and inequality of opportunity.'...It is not hard to notice that the task the Nehru had identified remains, alas, largely unaccomplished" (Dreze and Sen, 1996: 1). The executive wing of the state also performed below satisfaction to maintain law and order of the land and protect its citizens from powerful but mischievous forces.

On the other hand, the world's largest written constitution was amended nearly 100 times, 3194 bills were passed and the government promulgated 569 ordinances at the end of the 13th Lok Sabha (2003). All in the name of providing good governance. These are examples of legislative business undertaken by the government to effectively perform the executive functions and to make laws.

MP Fund Scheme: which side of the fence?

It is evident from the discussion of the functioning of the three wings of the state that the boundaries were neither closed nor fixed. More and more porous points emerged on these boundaries over the years. The borders are also expanding and taking new shapes. Under such circumstances, the MP Fund scheme locates itself in all spheres- the executive, the legislative and the judiciary. The MPs, as legislatures, design and modify the scheme guidelines, allot financial resources by passing the 'Budget' and 'Vote on Account'. They implement and execute the scheme either directly or indirectly. Any individual or agency that does not follow their instructions is punished, either legally or illegally.

5
Local Need

Belarasen also known as Barbarik a young warrior, wanted to end the Mahabharata battle within no time, contrary to the wishes of Lord Krishna. Therefore, he was not allowed to participate in the battle, but was given an opportunity to watch the great battle fought between the *Pandavas* and *Kauravas*. In the end, Belarasen rejected claims by the *Pandavas* and other warriors that they killed the largest number of enemies and are thus, responsible for winning the war. He revealed all that he saw was a "chakra", a weapon, which annihilated each and every body. The "chakra" in reality is the "kala chakra" that rules the universe. Similarly, in a famous play titled "Taj Mahal Ka Tender", the four *minaret-* of the Taj Mahal are identified as chimneys by the pollution control inspector despite repeated explanation by the builder that these are mere decorative towers for enhancing the beauty of the monument. Considerable delay takes place to get clearance from the pollution control authorities. In the Mahabharata case, though the truth is one, ordinary people like us cannot see or realize it. In the Taj Mahal case, we are biased not to see the facts deliberately. Thus the objective of exploring the psychics of the MPs to find out their intensions and actions with regard to projects selected under the MP Fund scheme is not only difficult but complex too. However, in this chapter, an attempt has been made to find out the reasons behind selecting particular types of projects by the MPs, their priorities and execution style. Of course, the attempt is to explore the half-truth, as we are not Belarasen.

First, we examine hundreds of projects undertaken under the MP Fund scheme to find out their true nature. Secondly, we try to explore the complexities in knowing the local and community requirements. And finally we try to find out the motives of the MPs in selecting a particular work instead of some other.

Characteristics of Projects

The Members of Parliament under the MPLADS had spent Rs. 12,176 crore as on end May 2005. Let us scan the list of permitted works as well as non-permitted projects funded by the MPs to find out their varieties, and characteristics (Annexure 5.1). We also scan the types of projects in which the MPs are interested in and which one discussed in the Parliamentary Committee on MPLADS. Though these projects need not, in the end, be supported by these Committees, these lists throw enough insight in to the MPs preferences (Annexure 5.2 and 5.3). These lists are prepared on the basis of studies conducted by the CAG, PEO, other studies by different institutions and individuals, mostly journalists.

1. All Possible Projects

Though the MPLADS guidelines provide a list of works that can or cannot be taken up, many projects undertaken are found to be outside the list. Of course this is not illegal. Taking up of a large number of projects that are prohibited is common for most of the MPs. It is also found that a few works, like construction of railway level crossing, which are permissible under the guidelines, are never taken up. All sorts of office and residential buildings, are constructed, and all types of repair work undertaken. Though most of the assets created are for community use, many are for individuals or small groups of beneficiaries. The officially reported names of the projects may not depict their true nature. There is a possibility that one may find something else at the field level. This is done to overcome the restrictions made under the official guidelines. The non-official guidelines are framed by all the stakeholders to suit the requirements of the beneficiaries. An illustrated list of projects is given below:

- Assets for religious entities like *Temples, Mosques, Churches and Gurudwaras* can be created by skillfully changing the names of the projects. For example, a *mandap* (platform) for a village community may actually be for a religious place.
- Officially the assets may be of projects allowed under the MPLADS guidelines, but in practice, the assets may be something totally different. Classrooms for schools may in reality be teacher quarters, a community hall may be a guest house for a government department.
- The assets may be created for a particular set of beneficiaries, but, the actual use may be different.

2. *Small projects*

PEO (2001) found that 46.41 percent of all the sample projects were small in nature as investment was less that Rs. 50,000 per project. Similarly 66.74 percent were below Rs. one lakh. Even in education and health, where the projects are basically for construction of classrooms, boundary walls or hospital buildings, the sizes of works were small (63.70% of school/ college buildings were below Rs. One lakh). Thus, the MPs opted for large number of small projects.

3. *Thrifty MPs*

The PEO observed, "most of the MPs while allocating fund to individual works seem to be thrifty despite the fact that there is a large unspent balance of MPLADS fund." (PEO, 2001: 18). The MPs allocate less funds for most of the projects based on their judgment of cost estimation. Sometimes, the "cost estimates are prepared afterwards and perhaps, made to conform to the amount allocated by the MP" (PEO, 2001: 18). The heads of 132 villages/wards out of 590 indicated that the funds were not allocated according to required costs and consequently many of the projects either remained incomplete or led to creation of poor quality assets (PEO 2001: 43).

4. *Maintenance of the assets neglected*

The MP Fund scheme does not have provision for separate maintenance component within the total allocation. The responsibility is on the head of the institutions and agencies that get the benefit. "Maintenance and upkeep of assets seem to have received less attention than it deserves. In fact, nobody seems to know how and by whom the assets are being looked after. The most question, which arise here, is how could an asset created under MPLADS be durable if there is neither a well defined mechanism to maintain it nor is there any fund specially provided for the same" (PEO, 2001: 47 & 63).

5. *Predecessors recommended projects supported by existing MPs*

Any project that was recommended by the predecessor MP may be taken up, if the present MP agrees to the proposal. In most of the cases, the latter respect the 'predecessor MPs' recommendations. Ninety one per cent MPs reported to have given their concurrence to all the pending works of their predecessors (PEO, 2001: 22).

6. *Popular Projects*

MP Fund scheme is the most popular development programme of the government. In other schemes, the divide between the actual beneficiaries and the implementing agencies and officials is quite big. Though in many of these schemes the peoples' representatives are involved, in practice, their contribution is very limited due to imperfect Panchayati Raj Institutions. But in case of MPLADS, the general public has better chance of getting a hearing from the MPs. Also, the PRI representatives influence the MPs more effectively to get many works executed. The PEO found that "nearly three-fourths of the sample works had originated from either the Panchayat Executives or the Municipal Councilors" (PEO, 2001: 58). Even local people (82%) know the executing agencies that are involved in execution of the projects, though they are ignorant of the details.

Characteristics of Local Need

Members of Parliament are peoples' representatives elected through either universal franchise (Lok Sabha) or indirectly (Rajya Sabha). They know the people, community, society and the geography of their constituencies. Thus, they can identify the local needs, which are complex, diverse, dynamic and unpredictable (Chambers, 1997). Before we identify the basic characteristics of the local needs, let us go through a few case studies that brought out in clear terms the peoples' reality. These case studies are culled out from hundreds of examples given by Robert Chambers in his 1997 book and Somesh Kumar in his 2002 book.

Low income the core problems

With the help of Participatory Rural Appraisal (PRA) methods, villages in Indonesia identified the 'low income' as their core problem. But in a Logical Framework Analysis (LFA in our chapter 2) or ZOPP/GOPP where the local community does not participate, the core problem identified was "natural resources in project area not used by the local population and government agencies in a sustainable way."

Water and sanitation the main priority

In Kilifi district in Kenya, a LFA/ZOPP exercise identified water and sanitation as the main priorities. But later, participatory appraisal and analysis found that the main priority was to empower the communities to manage their own developmental activities.

Ground rules for SHGs

The savings and credit self help groups (SHGs) are important local organisations all over the world, whose existence and growth are based on voluntary group participation. Hundreds of studies can be cited to identify suggestions to improve the working of the SHGs (rates of savings, application forms, eligibility, purpose of loan, rate of interest, repayment, penalties for default and credit ratio, etc.). But the minimum operational requirements for success of such SHGs as identified by a PRA exercise in south Indian villages are (i) transparent, accurate and honest accounting and (ii) that those with special responsibility are regularly rotated through democratic election and are not called president or secretaries but "representatives".

Dream of villages

In a village in Orissa, a dream map (a PRA tool) was drawn to reflect the way villagers would like their village to be in future. This helps planners to identify the "priority areas of change". The suggestions are (i) repair the check-dam to save the crop in summer, (ii) deepen the fish tank to rear fish, (iii) clean library premises and construct fence around it, (iv) arrest water stagnation around the tube-well, (v) straighten the village roads and bylanes, (vi) control certain diseases in the village, and (vii) solve the problem of unhygienic compost pit.

Genealogies and development work

Different groups participate differently in local development projects. The dominant groups are influential enough to corner the benefits of government-sponsored welfare and development schemes. Thus these groups must be identified to delimit developmental activities. A participatory genealogy method (a PRA tool) in Banswara district of Rajasthan found that the members of the main lineage (that started about 4-5 generations earlier) were active participants in development project and social activities in the village.

School vacation

A seasonal diagram method of PRA was conducted with a group of youth and school children in a village in Nigeria. Interestingly, the children suggested the shifting of vacation from the month of August (a happy month) to the months of June-July (saddest months on account of higher workload at the farm and lack of food and cash at home).

Poverty

Probably the most favourite subject for study by social scientist is on poverty. This also provides the most attractive remunerations to thousands of development professionals.

Worlds'most influential and rich institutions like World Bank, International Monetary Fund, Asian Development Bank, IFAD, DFAD, national planning bodies and commissions and multinational NGOs are in the business of poverty alleviation. This is clear from the book *Lords of Poverty*, authored by a former World Bank official Graham Hancook. Development professionals never agree while defining poverty and fail miserably while attempting to measure the number of poor. Identifying the causes and effects of poverty is becoming complex day-by-day and ranking them, next to impossible. However, left to themselves, the local communities (rural and urban) have proved that they can define poverty in their own terms and suggest remedial measures by identifying and ranking cases and effects. This is amply demonstrated by the village youth and women of Benue state in Nigeria, who perceived poverty in socio-psychological terms, like, lack of recognition, not being allowed to speak in public and the ability to attend burials, so important to the society. They identified 14 causes and 16 effects of poverty and also ranked them in descending order of importance. The most important causes were identified as laziness and illness. Effects identified included "wife may leave", "jealousy" and "always at home".

Land alienation

Social scientists and development professionals have probably left handy any scope to introduce any new dimension to the concept of land alienation. Lawmakers as well as law enforcers are busy for years to control the spread of land alienation. Even many extremist groups (naxalites and Landlords army Ranvir Sena in Bihar.) justify their existence to land alienation in poor rural communities. But the realities for local population as perceived by themselves found to be different. In a cause-effect diagram drawing exercise in Bolangir district of Orissa, the locals not only identified land alienation as a major issue but also rank the causes for that in order of intensity. The most intense cause was laziness and lack of earning leading to land mortgage, others being scarcity of rains resulting in crop failure leading to penury and lack of food, and the need of money for marriage of daughters, medical treatment and construction.

Illiteracy and education

In developing countries like India, illiteracy is a mass phenomenon and its magnitude is quite high particular disadvantaged sections – the scheduled castes, the scheduled tribes, nomadic communities, women, minorities and the poor. Commenting on India's National Education Policy, economist Jean Dreze and Amartya Sen opine that "The lamentable history of post-independent education policy has suffered from diverse kinds of inconsistencies and contradictions, including (1) a confusion of objectives, (2) inconsistencies between stated goals and actual policy, and (3) a specific contradiction between stated goals and resource allocation" (Dreze and Sen, 1996: 120). Their observations are for the whole country and may be different from the problem of illiteracy as perceived by the local communities. For example, villagers in Anantpur district in Andhra Pradesh identified the problem of illiteracy as the stem of the tree and the roots as ill-health causing irregular attendance; lack of money for bag, uniform, books; inadequate aid from government; illiterate parents not taking any interest in the education of their children; children engaged as child labourers and in performing household chores; teachers not interested in teaching and not attending to absenteeism of the children. They also came up with solutions to improve literacy and education.

Section and sub-section within a community

The village and local committees are not homogenous. So all the policies and programmes implemented by the government and other agencies for the benefit of a particular community or area may not reach all sections equally. "Ganda" is a community in western Orissa considered low in the social order. But in a well-being ranking exercise of this community in Tankarupara village of Bolangir district, five sub-sections were identified in 15 houses.

Village level worker (VLW)

Under the agricultural extension system of training and visit (T&V), sponsored and promoted by the World Bank, the

VLW is a key actor. VLWs are expected to stay close to the farmers and visit them frequently to help them adopt new methods of agricultural practices. But in a venn diagram method of PRA in a western Orissa village Ghantabahal, it was found that the VLW, as an institution, is not only less important for the villagers but also inaccessible.

Migration

Many people migrate to urban areas and other regions due to various reasons. Migrant unskilled workers and labourers live in urban slums. As per 2001 census, 40.6 million persons live in slums in 607 towns and cities and comprise 22.8 per cent of the population of these urban areas. This aspect is analysed by demographers in a push-pull dualistic paradigm. There are village specific factors that push the villagers out of their habitation and there are another urban specific set of factors that pull them out. But only the local communities and individual migrants know the exact factors that compel them to leave their homes. In a drought-prone village (Gurla Ura) in Bolangir district of Orissa, drought and landlessness emerged as the most important forces inducing migration. The most important inhibiting forces identified are emotional attachment to village and the excess workload during the migration. Surprisingly, this Force Field Analysis method found hardly any pull-factor in the eight "inducing forces" and nine "inhibiting forces".

Seed and crop choices

The choice of technology in agriculture as perceived by the farmers-the adopters-differs significantly from that of the scientists-the technology developers. Seed, one of the most critical inputs in agriculture attracts the attention of scientists the most. In a PRA study in Medak district of Andhra Pradesh, the preference for red gram varieties by women farmers revealed the differences between the farmers and the scientists. The scientists' nine criteria normally are: seed size, grain quality, days to maturity, seed colour, plant height, pest resistance, grain yield, protein content and cooking time. The farmers have additional criteria, a different perspective and a detailed interpretation and method while selecting a particular variety of red gram. Their twelve criteria are: height of plant, ability to intercrop, flower production, pod production, pod filling, pest damage by the pod borer, grain yield, wood bio-mass, quality of wood for construction, taste of grain, storability and grain price in local market. Similarly, the preferences for crop cultivation may differ even between male and female farmers. This was evident in Aukpa-Adoka village in Nigeria where it was observed that the male farmers preferred to cultivating yam but the female farmers prefer red pepper. The divide is so much that "the men do not cultivate pepper. If any man did so, he would be looked down upon. The women alone do it" (Kumar, 2002: 268).

Open defecation vs. sanitary latrine

The opening sentences of the guidelines on Central Rural Sanitation Programme (total sanitation campaign) read: Individual health and hygiene is dependent largely on adequate availability of drinking water and proper sanitation. There is therefore a direct relationship between water, sanitation and health.

A "demand driven approach" was adopted with increased stress on creating awareness and generating demand from the people for sanitary facilities in houses and schools and for cleaner environment. The emphasis was on health-and-hygiene related awareness through information, education and communication. This was supposed to change the preference of rural people from open defecation to sanitary latrine. This approach neglected the people's preference keeping in view encouraging and discouraging factors that are more diverse and complex. For example, the encouraging factors in order of importance were: no longer required to visit the foul-smelling bushes full of snakes; roofed latrines protect from rains; convenience during night; guests cannot be taken to the bushes; and nearness to home. The discouraging factors were: fear of pit-slab collapsing in rainy season; bad smell inside latrines without sanitary pipes; small size of the latrines; and the leakages of roofs in rainy season. Force Field Analysis showed that for the villagers of Odubwa in Nigeria, health and hygiene is not a deciding factor. This may be true for Indian villagers as well.

The case studies that were given in the preceding sections are a few examples out of thousands that bring out the basic nature of the local and community realities. To quote Chambers:

> "Many poor people's realities are local, complex, diverse, dynamic and unpredictable. For farming, forest-based and pastoral livelihoods, they often seek security by complicating and diversifying activities, and multiplying linkages and supports to exploit varied and varying local resources and opportunities. The value and preferences of poor local people typically contrast with those of the better off, outsiders and professionals. They need and want to be able to take a long view. They can, locally, manage greater complexity. Their values, preferences and criteria are typically numerous, diverse and dynamic and often differ from those supposed for them by professionals. Local people are themselves diverse, with sharp contrasts of preferences and priorities by age, gender, social and ethnic group and wealth."
>
> *(Chambers, 1997: 162)*

Communities need assessment: the techniques

In spite of complex, diverse, dynamic and unpredictable nature of local community needs, professional as well as amateur social scientists, technocrats, bureaucrats and policy planners do not refrain from adopting various techniques and tools to assess the local needs of the rural and urban communities. Their behaviour is basically dominating, lecturing and extracting. Their professionalism is limited to putting men before women, targeting achievement, setting priorities and transferring technology by simplifying packages. Their organizational system is bureaucratic, centralized, standardized and controlled. Career is the top priority for them and they rely on the formal education system to learn about the outside world. In the process, they adopt questionnaire survey methods to measure and arrive at facts that are statistically significant but may not be important for local communities. Let us discuss a few techniques used by development professionals to assess the local and community need, though their usefulness is always questionable. The first five techniques are drawn from Keith A Carter and Lionel J. Beaulieu (1992).

Key Informant approach

An interview or survey is conducted to elucidate information from a limited number of key informants, who may include professionals, elected officials, and heads of local institutions and public and social service organizations.

Public Forum approach

Group discussions are conducted to elicit information from a wide range of community members. Either all members of the community are involved or sizeable representative sections participate. They are asked to identify most important needs of the community and the steps they want to take to meet the needs.

Nominal Group Process approach

This takes place in a face-to-face non-threatening environment. The participants are in small groups "The nominal group process is intended to maximize creative participation of group members. Input from all participants is required. The process takes advantage of each person's knowledge and experience. This approach is useful in generating and clarifying ideas, reaching consensus, prioritizing and making decisions on alternative actions" (Carter and Beaulieu, 1992).

Delphi technique

This is similar to Nominal Group Process approach conducted in a non-face-to-face interaction environment in a workshop setting. A set of formal questionnaire focusing on identified issues, problems, causes, solutions and actions are developed for the individuals of the group. The answers are circulated and feedback summarized. The process continues till one is satisfied that the local needs are identified.

Structured Survey approach

An interview schedule or questionnaire is designed with a set of structured questions to elicit information from target respondents. The questions are mostly close-ended (alternative answers are given), straight and simple. They are given to individual respondents chosen carefully through a sampling procedure. Their survey may include personal interviews, questionnaires, telephonic interviews and mailers. The filled up questionnaires are analysed to find out the local community needs. This methodology is adopted by both the PEO and CBGA for evaluation of MPLADS. The latter even came to the conclusion that "contrary to ideal situation, nowhere in our sample constituencies, the selection of works were need based and nowhere, proper research was done to assess the needs before the MPs recommended works to the DCs" (Mohanty, 2004: 44).

All the above five methods have advantages and disadvantages. But, their performance as techniques and tools to identify and prioritise local community needs are in doubt. Thus other types of information gathering techniques are used aimed at overcoming the shortcomings of the survey methods. Two main classes of such methods- participatory observation and research, and participatory research and action, are discussed in brief.

Participatory Observation and Research

The main problem with the earlier techniques is that these are inadequate to capture complex situations and processes. In order to capture process-oriented activities, social scientists adopted a sort of participant observer approach that is inductive, selective and interpretative. This approach provides a framework for negotiating meanings, agreements and validating policy or development approaches and resolving differences. Commenting on this type of method (process documentation research and process monitoring) David Mosse wrote, "where interests are least entrenched or polarized, information has more of the characteristics of a 'public good'; where interests are deeply opposed, information production and use will be strongly linked to individual and collective political strategies. Process monitoring (and documentation), perhaps, has a definable niche within a spectrum of interest-formation links, occupying that place where interests are least polarized, where development outcomes have positive sum characteristics and where information is more like a public good separable from private interests" (Mosse, 1998: 50)

Participatory Research and Action

All the methods, techniques and tools that are adopted, primarily the first five categories, are subject to skeptical bias (accessible place near the main road), personal bias (outsiders view), elite bias (formally educated man in position), male bias, users/adopters bias (service providers discuss mainly with clients) and biases of the active, adult, present and able-bodied. We can add to this seasonal, timing, diplomatic, professional and project biases. Thus a set of participatory information collection methods are applied to know the local community needs. These methods also help community empowerment and collective actions. The list includes:

- Agro Ecosystem Analysis (AEA)
- Beneficiary Assessment (BA)
- Diagnostic Rural Participative (DRP)
- Farmers Participatory Research (FPR)
- Participatory Appraisal of Natural Resources (PANR)
- Participatory Action Research (PAR)
- Participatory Analysis and Learning Methods (PALM)
- Participatory Appraisal (PA)
- Participatory Learning and Action (PLA)
- Participatory Rapid Rural Appraisal (PRRA)
- Participatory Rural Appraisal (PRA)
- Participatory Urban Appraisal (PUA)
- Visualisation in Participatory Programme (VIPP)
- Rapid Rural Appraisal (RRA)
- Rapid Ethnographic Assessment (REA)
- Rapid Participatory Rural Appraisal (RPRA).

Robert Chambers advocated PRA and claimed its superiority in assessing local community needs compared to questionnaire survey and semi-structured interviews.

Table 5.1

	Verbal (interview, conversation etc.)	*Visual (map, model, matrix, diagram, etc.)*
Outsider's mode and role	Probing investigator	Faciliating, initiator and catalyst
Insider's mode and style	Reactive respondent	Creative analyst and presenter
Investigative style	Extractive	Performative
Insider's awareness of outsider	High	Low
Eye contract	High	Low
The medium and materials are those of	Outsider	Insider
Detail influenced by	Etic categories	Emic categories
Information flow	Sequential	Cumulative
Accessibility of information to others	Low transient	High semi-permanent
Initiative for cross-checking	Outsider	Insider
Ownership of information	Appropriated by outsider	Shared, can be owned by insider
Utility for complex analysis	Low	High

Source: Chambers (1997), Page 150.

PRA method may be the suitable tool (map, model, metric, diagram etc.) to identify local needs. But the philosophy behind this approach does not advocate generalizing and aggregating the findings. This implies nearly six lakh villages and many more habitations and communities in India are difficult to cover through PRA. PRA's aim of building consensus and plan for collective action is difficult to achieve given the geographical spread of the country. Where is the money, time, initiative catalyst and infrastructure to conduct nationwide PRA in all the villages and find out local needs and plan of action to satisfy them. Secondly, when information is not a public commodity, the social structure is shaped by the power structure of the community and every event is the outcome of a disequilibrium process under such a situation, participatory appraisal methods, including PRA, do not provide all the answers.

Local Communities Need Assessment and Action: The Political Approach

In the previous sections it is established that the local community needs are complex, dynamic, diverse and unpredictable. It is also realized that the methods, techniques and tools applied to access local community needs are inadequate, deficient, and at times, archaic. One can try to apply sophisticated statistical, anthropological and participatory methods and spend money, time and resources, but the success rate may not be optimal. Development practitioners of all types have failed the country and the people in the past years, at least in local area development. The bureaucratic development professional-managed local area development is conceptualized in Diagram1.

Diagram 1

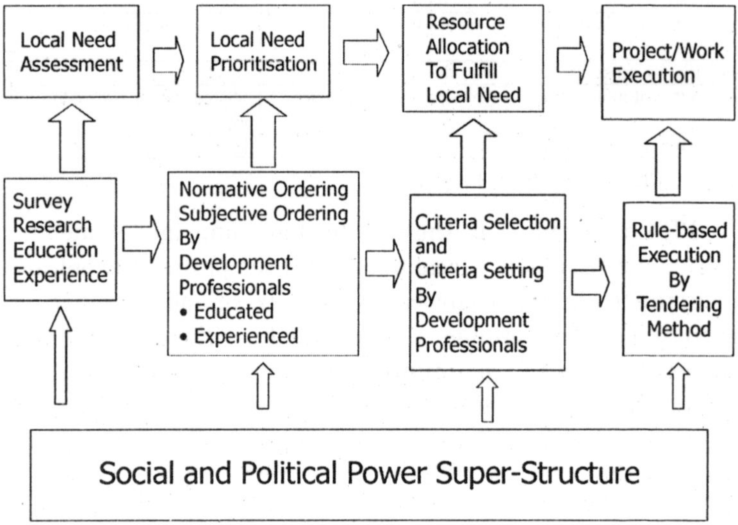

Development professionals in a bureaucratic framework try to find out local needs and also priorities them based on their educational backgrounds and experience (normative/subjective). The criteria are chosen to make the process theoretically transparent, indiscriminately, just and efficient. But in practice, the criteria are designed to meet the needs of the powerful stakeholders. Even at the time of prioritization of various types of local needs, the powerful stakeholder influences the process. Lastly, at the time of execution, rule-based procedures are followed in the name of financial prudence and accountability, even though this may not be the most efficient and economical way to achieve the target. One can say that development professionals do not even know about local needs, their prioritization being a distant goal. Secondly, the rule-based and criteria-based resource allocation and works execution is subjected to all sorts of biases and manipulation. So, let us examine another type of local area development model adopted and executed under the MP Fund scheme. Before that, the considerations based on which an MP allots funds for different types of projects are examined (Diagram 2).

Diagram 2

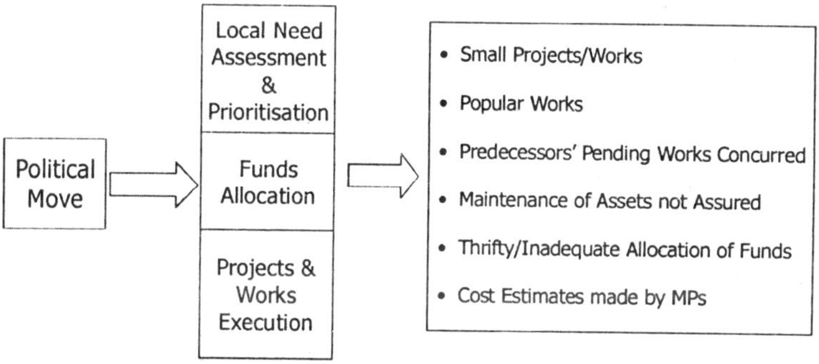

Most MPs want to continue in the next term. For this their parties need to form government to wield power. So, MPs adopt various strategies to win votes. Thus assessment of local needs and prioritizing them is based on their knowledge of constituencies and political priorities.

The projects are generally smaller in nature so that to meet the needs of a large number of groups. The more of them can be approved projects are popular in the sense that they make a larger section of the population happy though they may not be useful. In electoral politics, every vote counts and every section is important. Nobody should be dissatisfied. So, projects selected by the predecessor MPs are also given importance to gain some political mileage. The MPs are not worried about the maintenance of the assets created as it required more funds. The voting behavior of people is influenced more by the creation of an asset but not its maintenance. Once a project is executed and an asset created, it becomes the main determinant in elections. More initiation of a project is sufficient in a few cases to attract enough votes. And this is the reason why MPs allot inadequate funds for a project; at times completion of a project is not even included in the plan. The local community's need assessment as made under this scheme and the action taken therein is depicted in Diagram 3. This model is for all political representatives elected directly like the MPs, MLAs and the PRI representatives.

Diagram 3

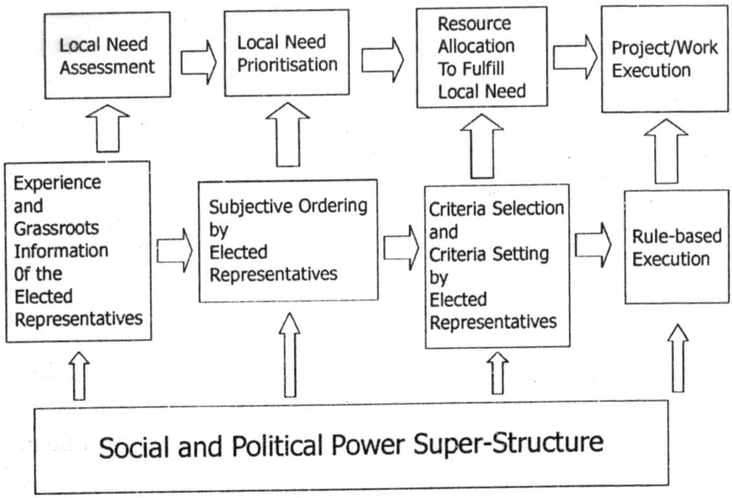

Democracy and Development

A comparison between the development – professional way at local community and area development and the political way should not automatically favour one over the other. For maximizing gains from either of the systems, an enabling environment as well as a controlling environment must be in place. Much of the criticism of these two systems arises due to a lack of enabling environment on one hand, and an undeveloped and deficient controlling environment on the other. Before we specify the nature and ingredients of these two environments, we have to understand the development process in a democracy. For us, development process means economic development in terms of improvement in the well being of the citizens at large. Rise in per capita income, poverty alleviation, reduction in social disparities are a few important components of this development process.

Many social analysts think electoral democracy is not suitable for poverty alleviation. To prove this point, Ashutosh Varshney has shown that poverty levels are high in several poor countries that have been following democratic governance for decades (India: 35% below poverty line, Sri Lanka: 25%, Philippines: 37.5%, Jamaica: 34.2%, Trinidad: 21%, Costa Rica: 22%, Venezuela: 33% and Botswana (1986): 33%). The reason because, says Varshney, democracy encourages direct rather than indirect attacks on poverty. And since direct attacks are less effective than indirect attacks, poverty falls only slowly (Aiyer, *ToI*, ND, 20 Sept., 2001). For getting vote, direct measures are more attractive and visible than indirect measures, but, the effectiveness in terms of poverty reduction is more in case of indirect measures. In India, the elected representatives at village, block, district, state and nation level have to play specific roles in designing and implementing various poverty alleviation measures: both direct and indirect. One can also observe the competition between these elected representatives in taking the credit for these steps. While MPs and MLAs allocate huge money for poverty reduction schemes, the actual work is done by the Panchayat representatives at village and local community level. And this is probably the reason for MPs and MLAs to demand direct role in allocation of funds for local area development as well as its execution. This situation is depicted in Table 5.2.

The direct attack on poverty through subsidies, food distribution, job reservation, land reforms (qualified), cheap credit policy, employment guarantee, food-for-work and many such instruments are majoritarian in nature. Aiyar observed that "democracies are majoritarian rather than equalitarian...what economists regard as leakages of entitlements to the non-poor

Table 5.2
Politics of Direct and Indirect Attack on Poverty

Attack on Poverty	*Result on Poverty Alleviation*	*Nature*	*Politician's Role*	*Types of Politicians in control*
Direct 1. Subsidies 2. Food distribution 3. Job reservation 4. Land reform 5. Loan scheme like IRDP/SGSY	Less effective	1. Visible to voters 2. Majoritarian	Support	Panchayati Raj representative Members of Legislative Assemblies (MLAs)
Indirect 1. Accelerate GDP growth 2. Productivity growth of factors of productions 3. Market friendly policy 4. Public investment in health & education	Effective in long run	1. Invisible to voters 2. Not majoritarian	No support	Members of Parliament (MPs)

are not really seen as leakages at all by politicians. It makes sense for politicians to propose entitlements that benefit the majority of the population rather than the poorest 30 percent. This explains why politicians happily subsidise water, electricity, fertilizer and food for all income groups, and provide job reservation for castes accounting for up to 85 per cent of the population in some States" (Aiyer, *ToI*, New Delhi, 2 Sept., 2001). Commenting on this type of majoritarian strategy, Drize wrote "...a recent proposal to expand the Integrated Child Development Services (ICDS) was 'categorically rejected' by the Cabinet, on the grounds that there was 'no money'. Meanwhile, lavish resources are spent to placate the more influential sections of society– private corporations, the military establishment, public employees, and all so-called 'middle classes', among others". He also pointed out that "as a ratio of GDP, public expenditure on health in India is among the lowest in the world about one per cent". (Drize, *The Hindu*, ND, 12 March, 2004).

Answering to a question on China leaving India behind, Manmohan Singh, the architect of India's economic reforms, opined, "May be it is the result of democracy. Before politicians can become statesmen, they want to be re-elected. That shortens their horizon. But without long-term visions, this country's development potential cannot be realized" (ToI, New Delhi, 16 July, 2001). But there are scholars who think otherwise. Amartye Sen thinks, "despite the generalization that democracy tends to slow down economic growth, extensive cross-country comparisons have not provided any empirical support for this apt-repeated belief...The basic point is that economic growth is helped by the friendliness of the economic climate, rather than by the fierceness of the political regime. If India has failed to do enough to create such a favorable climate and was unable to learn from the positive experiences of China or South Korea, the blame can hardly be put on the shoulders of political freedom of citizens. Indeed, more engaging public discussion on what needs to be done can help to charge India's deficiencies. This calls for more democracy not less" (Sen, 2004).

Restriction and Boundaries

The MPs as people's representatives, elected through a universal franchise, try for the social and economic development of their constituencies. They follow different paths as politicians. They follow different political thoughts. The categories are: socialist (you have two cows- you give one to your neighbors), communist (you have two cows, the government takes them both and gives you the milk), Fascist (you have two cows, the government takes both and sells you the milk), Nazis (you have two cows, the government takes both and shoots you), capitalist (you have two cows- you sell one and buy a bull) and trade unionist (you have two cows, they take them from you, shoot one, milk the other and throw the milk away). The moral is: MPs only want to be in power. And in a democratic country like India, voters are the medium to gain and wield power. Thus they and their political parties apparently follow different strategies to enrich the living conditions of the voters. At the national level, as discussed in the previous section, the political parties (and their representatives) follow multiple strategies to get more votes by ensuring higher economic growth, employment, minimum price rise, higher income and many other benefits. Similarly, for local area and community development they follow various strategies. In so far as the model they follow to use MP fund was explained in preceding sections. Theoretically, local community development by elected representatives probably follows the most suitable path as in case of MP Fund scheme. But its efficiency level can be improved by adopting a few management and governance practices.

Let the Fund be lapsable

This is the only scheme run by the government of India where the financial allocation to a MP is non-lapsable. This kind of arrangement helps the MPs to stagger the expenditure nearing the election time. This results in unutilisation of funds within a short period. The PEO also recommended that "the unspent balance of the predecessor MP should lapse... These procedural changes will prevent accumulation of unspent balance without effecting the development under the scheme" (PEO, 2001: xii). The MPs then will be serious to spend the fund in time.

Transparency in scheme implementation

Information on the projects, their cast and names of the implementing agencies and contractors should be publicized widely through both the print and electronic media. Local news papers and radio and TV stations should be used to disseminate MP Fund - related information. The voters of the parliamentary constituency would act as pressure groups. By this the MPs can not afford to ignore the needs of the community. A particular region of a constituency may not get disproportionately large sum of MP Fund under such a transparent system.

ANNEXURE 5.1

Type/Nature of projects undertaken by MPs under the MPLADS (compiled from the report of the Comptroller and Auditor General of India: 1998)

Providing additional distribution transformers, Renovation of roads, Special repair of Dargah path, Drilling and commissioning of tube wells, Renovation of old water supply lines, Providing new sewerage line, Construction of school building, Cricket pavilion, Panchayat Ghar, Mettalled roads, Pavment of streets, Water supply scheme, Mahila mandal/ yuvak mandal bhawan, Irrigation channels, Playground, Village authority court, Construction of bridges, Approach roads, Beautification of Custom House building, Building of cultural centres, Library cum community centres, High schools, Colleges, Indoor sport complex, Health centres, Footpaths, Cooperative sugar Ltd., Labour services cooperative society, Sanghas, Clubs, Ashrams, Construction of buildings for Registered Society and Private Christian Hospital, Works relating to private Charitable Hospital, Roads of Housing Society, Library of District bar association, Post literacy cum vocational training centre, Mandapam owned by temple trust board, Godown for handloom weavers cooperative society, Fishermen cooperative society, Compound wall to TMCA playground.

Type/Nature of projects undertaken by MPs under the MPLADS (Compiled from the Report of the Comptroller and Auditor General of India: March 2000)

Construction of bridges, OHSRs RWS Schemes, Roads, Causeway and Culverts, Schools, Library building in women college, ST bus stand, Water supply, Works of small buildings, Bridge at Kochianala, Construction of rooms in schools, Retaining wall, Silver Jubilee building in Dr. Ambedkar Government arts College at Vyasarpadi, College building, Construction of auditorium at Bishnupur and Dumnisol bridge under Joypur Panchayat Samiti (Annex-VI of CAG Report:2000)

Construction of municipal building, Payment of electrical charges, Shifting of power lines, Purchase of computers, Salaries of employees, Building materials procured, Utilised for execution of JRY, diverted to Employment Affirmation Scheme, Diverted to Personnel Deposit Account, Diverted to Post Office Saving Account (Annex- VII of CAG Report: 2000)

Construction of houses for weaker section, Construction of works of Government offices, Construction of Police Beat, Stadium at SSB Centre, Computer room, Building for Police personnel, PWD Inspection Bungalow, Doctor's recreation and office building, Panchayat Ghars, PWD rest house, Community hall for Police, Office for Government LPS, Building at Police line, Police Training Centre, Courts, Beautification/ renovation/ fencing/ boundary wall of DC's offices, SDO's quarters, Waiting hall at Courts, Boundary walls at Police Station, Rest-shed at Collector's residence, Development work of Prithni Raj Smarak, Construction of Panchayat Bhawan, Faryadi Pratikshalaya, Railing to bridges/ stadium/ swimming pool, Construction of indoor stadium in government premises (Annex- VIII of CAG Report: 2000).

Construction of private and commercial institutions, Youth clubs, Youth building, Computer centre etc., Construction of private garden, Private school,, Clubs, Samilti, and computer training centre, Works of private trusts/ institutions, Officer's club, Kalyan Mandap, Establishment of floriculture and horticulture farms, Construction work at Aurobindo Institute of Art and Culture, Construction of halls for Gorkha Youths, Nari Samaj, MHIP, YMA, MUP and computers to Zonal Audio Visual Institution, Setting of PCOs/ shops/ private clinics, Individual farms, Press club, Bus stand, Bar association building, DJ courts, Construction of commercial complexes, Milk Production societies, Construction of Tripura road Transport Corporation complex, Construction of stalls and spinning centre, Construction of unrecognised/ unaided schools, library building in private schools, private ashrams, motel and bar associations, Mahurar association, Mahila Mandal building, Boy hostel for RK Mission, Construction of Rehra stands and Labour sheds in various sectors, Provision of computer to Centre for Tourism Studies, Sheds for Sarvodaya Sangh, Silk Weavers (Annex- IX of CAG Report: 2000).

Repair of roads & school buildings etc., Renovation of Kala Krishti Sangh, Repair and extension of inspection bungalow, Repair and Kutcha works, Resurfacing of raods, ponds, parks, Maintenance and allowances for computer instructors in schools, Wire-fencing, Levelling of fields, Footpath repair, Providing pipe water connection, Providing shingling for maintenance and improvement of inter-village roads, Repair of streets, Drains, dharmshalas, Repair and deepening of wells, Repair of pensioners association quarters, Street lightings (Annex- X of CAG Report: 2000).

Purchase of ambulances, Hearse vans, Hospital equipments, Water coolers, Computer for district Panchayats, Screw-air compressor, Ambulance for an association and Aggrawal sabha, Purchase of materials for victims of militancy, Tipper vehicle, Books POL etc., Vehicle for Municipal Council, CTV sets for Arts club, Multimedia projector for police, Mortuary van, Purchase of furniture for schools, Books for Bar Associations, Purchase of generation sets, motor & pipes, motor pump sets, Sub-mercible motors, Tata Sumo vehicle for medical college, Sodium lamps, TV sets for panchayats, 75 HP Engine for Aliar Dam, Purchase of water tankers, Pollution testing machine, Books, (Annex- XI of CAG Report: 2000).

Construction of porters track, mule-track, and improvement of porters tracks, Beautification of parks, Electrical amenities in other than slum areas, Widening of railway crossing, Fish farm, Construction of chabutaras, Deepening of canals, Formation of thrashing floors, Gravelling works, Providing Internet lease connections to nodal Centres for High Schools, Temporary earth works, Acquisition of land, Retro reflective boards, MS boards, Ornamental lighting and beautification of city (Annex- XIII of CAG Report: 2000).

Broad Categories of completed Works undertaken by MPs under the MPLADS (Compiled from the Evaluation Report on MPLADS, PEO, Planning Commission: November 2001)

- Roads and Bridges (30.78% of works in this sector)

- Irrigation (3.058% of works in this sector)
- Drinking water and sanitation (11.78% of works in this sector)
- Community works (22.89% of works in this sector)
- Education (19.00% of works in this sector)
- Health (1.92% of works in this sector)
- Others (10.58% of works in this sector)

ANNEXURE 5.2

Suggestions made by the XIIIth Lok Sabha Members for works and other issues (collected from various reports of the Committee on MPLADS: 1st Report, May 2000 to 11th Report, April 2004)

Allowing audio-visual aids under MPLADs to benefit the student community. Such items may include purchase of colour TV, video cassettes, video cassettes players, video cassettes recorder.

Nominated members have represented that they should be allowed to recommend works throughout the country.

Inclusion of items connected with railway passenger amenities in the illustrative list.

Creating computer centers - not only in government institutions and government aided institutions but also in government recognized institutions.

Specific provision may also be made in the guidelines to prevent assets which have been created from being transferred to or by any private body.

The proposal for proportionate increase in the allocation of MPLADS funds based on the population of voters in the constituency.

The committee further notes that MPLADS allocation per year per MP was doubled on 23rd December, 1998. Funds amounting to Rs. 2 crore are being released for each MP from the year 1998-99. The committee feels that this increased amount of Rs. 2 crore per year is just not sufficient to implement developmental schemes based on the locally felt needs of the constituents. The committee therefore recommends that the present allocation of Rs. 2 crore may be enhanced to Rs. 4 Crore.

Rs.10 lakh from MPLADS funds of every member be contributed towards Orissa cyclone relief.

Providing drinking water tankers and digging of bore wells to mitigate the sufferings of people in their constituencies, which come in the grip of extreme drought conditions.

Providing a vehicle to MP for inspection of works executed under MPLAD scheme.

Providing LPG cylinder and regulator to women below poverty line.

Purchase of artificial limbs and cycles for distribution to disabled persons under MPLADS.

Contribution of Rs. 5 Lakh out of MPLADS Funds for internet dhabas in all Block /Mandal Headquarters in the country recommend that funds should be provided for this purpose as it fell under the infrastructure category.

The committee note the supposal and recommend the position stated by the Ministry of Statistics and Programme Implementation in this regard that the works up to Rs. One lakh can be executed departmentally by state government agencies to avoid any delay.

Allowed for construction of community halls and community mandapams. Construction of buildings for mahila mandals can also be taken up.

Recommend that the panchayat offices should not be covered by this restriction,

Allow E-governance and development of related software under MPLADS would basically require allowing implementation of computers scheme in government offices which was not allowed at present.

Purchase of storage refrigerator for blood banks.

Construction of hall or auditorium. library building for bar association.

Construction of building of Lion's club and Rotary clubs subject to a ceiling of Rs. 5 lakh be raised to Rs. 10 lakh by making an amendment.

Distribution of MPLADS cheques to the beneficiaries under the MPLAD scheme.

Amend guidelines on MPLADS for inclusion of construction of boundary wall in the illustrative list of works.

Inclusion of registered societies and trusts and construction of blood bank projects in the illustrative list of works that can be taken up under MPLADS.

Proposal of five hon'ble members of Rajya Sabha for construction of a bridge across Vaigai river between Varusanaadu and Singarajapuram in Andipatti assembly constituency in Theni district of Tamil Nadu.

Construction of a railway level crossing at Chandanpur in the Howrah Burdwan chord line in the Howrah division of the eastern railway.

Purchase of consumable items like beds, bed- sheets and blankets as these are inventory items and purchase of which was specifically prohibited under the MPLADS guidelines.

Construction of buildings adjacent to religious places.

Construction of a railway over bridge costing Rs. 1 crore by providing Rs. 50 Lakh each for the year 2000-2001 and 2001-2002 at Dewas on Ujjain Bhopal road under MPLADS.

Making provision of 50 per cent contribution by state governments to each work to be taken up under MPLADS.

Treatment of major ailments for people below poverty line and for people who cannot afford major surgeries/ treatment.

Allowing computerization of villages through MPLADS in Rajapur parliamentary constituency (Maharashtra)

Construction of post offices.

Purchase of hospital equipment: allowing mobile vans with audio-visual arrangement: allowing audio- visual training for educational purposes: modern audio- visual systems for various types of sports and games.

Allowing essential items of furniture like ordinary beds, chairs, benches, etc., for common shelter / home and educational institutions.

Contribute any amount they desire up to rupees two crore for each natural calamity of rare severity in any part of the country.

Permission to utilise some money out of his quota of MPLADS funds for works outside his parliamentary constituency.

Construction of roads within premises of unaided but recognized institutions under MPLADS.

Utilization of Rs. one crore for execution of a minor irrigation project in his parliamentary constituency.

Inclusion of repair/maintenance of Gram Pravesh Dwars under MPLAD scheme.

Purchase of water tanker lorries out of MPLADS funds for local bodies.

Allocation of additional funds for construction and development of rural and link roads in their respective constituencies in addition to allocation under the MPLADS.

Relaxation beyond the limit of Rs. 25 lakh for construction of a Jasara bridge at the cost for Rs. 39 lakh under Singhee Gram Panchayat Samiti of Bolpur panchayat samiti in Bolpur parliamentary constituency of West Bengal.

Prevision of water takers for transportation of potable water to mitigate the hardships of their constituents in drought affected areas.

Contribute Rs. 25 lakh towards Orissa flood relief from his quota of MPLADS funds.

Relaxation in the limit of Rs. 25 lakh and entrusting the execution of works for construction of bridges and road in Andaman district to MES as per the choice of the hon'ble member.

Former and the present who have contributed from their quota of MPLADS funds should be invited at the time of inauguration of a work executed under the MPLAD scheme.

Installation of computers in Saraswati Shishu Vidya Mandir in Behrampur parliamentary constituency.

Contribution of Rs. 10 lakh under MPLAD scheme for the flood devastated areas of Palgher, Vasai Dahanu Talukas and Bhiwandi Taluka of Thane district in Maharashtra.

Purchase of a mobile Diagnostic centre- cum- Pathological clinic to hand it over to the NGO Bharat Sevashram Sangha in Serampore parliamentary constituency from MPLADS funds.

Inclusion of purchase of books, computer, furniture, curriculum based educational software and other items of infrastructure development in the government as well as private libraries.

Relaxation beyond the limit of Rs. 25 lakh under MPLADS Scheme for (a) construction of lecture hall- cum- class rooms (b) provision of computer, Server and other related accessories for the PC Lab (c) construction of library building (d) construction of laboratory building and (e) construction of hostel for Hooghly Engineering and Technology College, Pipulpati in Hooghly parliamentary constituency of Kolkatta and approve it.

Relaxation beyond the limit of Rs. 25 lakh for construction of Mata Gujri Public School of Mata Gujri Educational society Chak Suhele Wala in Ferozepur.

Relaxation beyond the limit of Rs.25 lakh for implementation of project costing Rs. 35 lakh- for "Pevanna Podivil Kadavu Tookupalam at Oorngatiri Panchayat.

Rs. 25 lakh for construction of railway under – bridge at Mukkali km. 719/7-8 on Calicut – Mangalore railway line in Badagore parliamentary constituency of Kerala.

NGOs/ implementing agencies for setting up modern kitchens for enabling them to involve themselves actively in making available the cooked meals to poor and needy children of schools in urban / rural areas for efficient implementation of the mid-day meal scheme.

The reputed NGOs, including managing committees of the educational institutions, can be the implementing agencies for the works under the scheme, if the district head considers them as capable of executing the works satisfactorily.

India support in the sector of non- conventional energy for solar energy projects in scheduled casts villages was concerned.

Purchase of mobile medical vans for Maharaj Agrasen Hospital , Punjabi Bagh.

Purchase of five battery operated open buses for Heritage City of Chandni Chowk.

Purchase of generators and refrigerators for government hospitals (public utility items for government hospitals).

Relaxation beyond the limit of Rs. 25 lakh for construction of a Jasara bridge at the cost for Rs, 39 lakh under Singhee Gram Panchayat Samiti of Bolpur panchayat Samiti in Bolpur parliamentary constituency of West Bengal.

ANNEXURE 5.3

Suggestions made by the Rajya Sabha Members for works and other issues (collected from the various reports of the committee on MPLADS: Rajya Sabha. 1st Report, December 1999 to 5th Report, November 2004)

Big Construction Works:

Enlarging the scope of the MPLAD scheme for allowing the railways to instal level crossings etc.

For construction of auditorium for Jawahar Lal Darda Institute of Engineering and Technology

Relaxation of certain conditions in MPLADS guidelines in respect of women polytechnic in Lucknow being set up by Vinod Gupta charitable foundation.

Construction of building for schools for rural technology and engineering.

Construction of FCI godowns for storage of food grains.

Construction of a seminar hall at Koneru Lakshmaiah College of Engineering, Vaddeswarum of Guntur district and a library at Vignan Engineering College, Vadlamudi of Guntur district, Andhra Pradesh for the allotment of funds from MPLADS over Rs. 25 lakhs.

40 lacs for construction of School of Physiotherapy building within the premises of V.S. General Hospital, Ahmedabad.

Relaxation of upper limit of Rs. 25 lakhs for individual works for construction of cultural centers under MPLADS funds.

Establishment of North East Regional Institute of Parliamentary Studies Training and Research (NERIPSTR) at Guwahati.

Construction of railway level crossing at Chandanpur in the Howrah-Burdwan chord line in the Howrah division of the eastern railway.

Construction of a bridge across Vaigai river between

Varusannadu and Singarajapuram in Andipatti assembly constituency in Theni district of Tamil Nadu.

Construction of a seminar hall at Koneru Lakshmaiah College of Engineering, Vadeswarum and a library at Vignan Engineering College, Vadlamudi both of Guntur district, Andhra Pradesh.

Construction of School of Physiotherapy building in V.S. General Hospital.

Construction of foot over bridge across the river Salandi in Orissa under MPLADS

Construction of Kolhapur type weir (water storage) on Rangavali river at Navapur district, Maharashtra under MPLADS.

Construction of foot over bridge near Govandi railway station, Chembur, Mumbai, Maharashtra.

Construction of an over-head tank at Rampur, Uttar Pradesh (costing Rs. 44 lakh).

Construction of roads and bridges in Andamans.

Construction of two bridges in Purnea parliamentary constituency.

Construction of hospital building for the proposed government Medical College at Latur costing Rs. 75 lakhs.

Construction of boy's and girl's hostel costing Rs. 95 lakhs each at Rajarshi Chattrapati Shahu Maharaj government Medical College, Kolhapur.

Utilisation of Rs. 1 crore for execution of a minor irrigation project in Deogarh, Orissa.

Providing financial assistance for construction of building for Shri Jain Medical and Educational Trust, Bhuj-Kutch.

Construction of a hospital block at Manjeri Distt., Malappuram, Kerala.

Construction of community hall/auditorium at Silchar costing about Rs. 3 crores.

Construction of School Complex "VISION – 2001" at Varlakanda – Lakshmisagara Villages of Gudibande Taluk, Kolar District, Karnataka.

Construction of railway over-bridge at Dewas on Ujjain-Bhopal road, Madhya Pradesh.

Contribution of Rs. 40 lacs for construction of School of Physiotherapy building within the premises of V.S. General Hospital, Ahmedabad

Construction of guest houses outside his constituency at Ernakulam and Kozhikode in Kerala and Mangalore in Karnataka.

Construct three bridges in Gwalior each costing over Rs. 50 lakhs.

Construction of third floor building at Jamia Hamdard, Hamdard University.

Construction of two bridges at an estimated cost of Rs. 37 lakhs and Rs. 67 lakhs.

Construction of first floor building of the Friend-in-need society, an old age home in Chennai, Tamil Nadu at an estimated cost of Rs. 35 lakhs.

Providing financial assistance for construction of building for Shri Jain Medical and Educational Trust, Bhuj-Kutch.

Construction Works

Construction of passenger amenities at railway stations under MPLADS Fund.

Construction of a memorial Community Hall under MPLADS.

Construction of guest houses outside the parliamentary constituency.

Erection of statue of Mahatma Gandhi in Trichur, Kerala out of the interest accrued on the MPLADS.

Incomplete buildings under MPLADS.

Utilization of MPLADS funds for special forestry project.

Construction of houses at Dholaveera Village in Gujarat under MPLADS (by a NGO).

Construction of shopping centers for village panchayats.

Construction of police beat at Naharlagun, Arunachal Pradesh.

Construction of post offices.

Computer and IT:

Embark upon exploring further areas like cateloguing of CD ROM Library, computer cateloguing of libraries in schools which the Committee feels can make school libraries more scientific and systematic so that books could be easily located on the shelf of the library without much loss of time. The cateloguing of CD ROM will also help school libraries in occupying less of space for housing large volume of informations on CDs and on the screens of the computer which may be helpful for the school teachers and students in citing information in less time.

Purchase of Computers for Government recognized institutions.

Relaxation of MPLADS guidelines for accommodating e-governance and software development.

Proposal for computer and internet facility to public library run by charitable trust, a new roof for a community hall run by village church and provision for 3-4 computers per school.

Proposal regarding installation of computers in libraries in his constituency.

Proposal of supply of computers to privately managed high schools recognized by the State Government.

Purchase of computers for Viklang Urban Co-operative Credit Society Ltd. Surat.

Computerization of villages in Rajapur parliamentary constituency, Maharashtra.

Purchase of tele-medicine system with video conferencing unit.

Inventory Items:

Interest accrued on MPLADS funds should be utilised for purchase of vehicles like jeep which are instrumental in monitoring the developmental activities as Members do a lot of touring thereof.

The Committee agreed for purchase of T.V. sets provided the concerned MP as well as concerned authority assessed whether there was a proper place and proper provision for safe custody for keeping these instrument under supervision of responsible persons of the concerned Institutions.

One time assistance to the proposal and emphasized on the condition that recurring cost of the system of the Night Soil Disposal system.

Permission to purchase mobile buses/vans under MPLADS.

Purchase of refrigerator for preserving blood in blood banks.

Utilization of MPLAD funds for providing drinking water tankers.

Release of LPG connections.

Request from NIF to MPs to allocate MPLADS fund towards scounting, spawning and sustaining grassroot innovations in their constituencies.

Funds for the purchase of books for the Library of the Bar Association at Patna.

Procurement of essential blood bank equipments for the Rotary Blood Bank in Delhi including purchase of blood mobiles with appropriate accessories for collection of blood.

Purchase of a bus for government girls degree college in Udhampur parliamentary constituency in Jammu and Kashmir.

Procurement of dental van under MPLADS.

Purchase of digitization equipment for Sundarayya Grandhalaya Samstha.

Suggestion regarding inclusion of purchase of rotating sprinklers under MPLADS.

Purchase of garbage collection vehicle under MPLADS.

Purchase of motor boats for flood and cyclone affected areas in Orissa.

Purchase of books and furniture for Pandit Shyamji Krishna Verma Public Memorial Trust, a Public Library at Mandvi.

Inclusion of purchase of Aqua-guard Coolers and drinking water tankers under MPLAD scheme.

Purchase of mammography machine for the Kidwai Memorial Institute of Oncology.

Purchase of literary books for distribution in school and public libraries.

Purchase of heart and lung machine in the Deptt. of Cardiovascular and Thoracic Surgery at J.J. Hospital, Mumbai (Rs. 52 Lakh).

Purchase of poclainer/escavator for creation of infrastructure for desilting of ponds, canals, donkas and for formation and maintenance of roads etc.

Launching of "Clean City Programme" and purchase of garbage collection vehicles.

Construction of Kolhapur type weir (water storage) on Rangavali river at Navapur District, Maharashtra under MPLADS.

Purchase of a bus for the trainees of a sports hostel, Ponda, Goa.

Purchase of Mammography Machine for the Kidwai Memorial Institutes of Oncology (Shri C.K. Jaffer Sharief, M.P.

Provision of equipments for gymnastic centres.

Purchase of literary books for distribution in schools and public libraries.

Distribution of sowing seeds to poor farmers due to drought conditions in Shimoga parliamentary constituency of Karnataka.

Purchase of ambulance equipped with laboratory equipment and other medical equipment which can be used as a mini operation theatre.

Repair Works:

Construction of boundary walls of schools, colleges and educational buildings community halls, cremation grounds, parks and gardens out of MPLADS funds.

Allowing repair/maintenance of 'Gram Pravesh Dwars' under MPLAD scheme.

Repair of school building of M.H. High School, Thane at a cost of Rs. 14.5 lakhs.

Repair of irrigation canal under MPLADS.

Natural Calamity:

Contribution of Rs. 10 lakhs from MPLADs funds for relief and reconstruction work in the flood hit state of Himachal, Pradesh.

Contribution of Rs. 25 lakhs for Orissa flood relief.

Utilization of MPLADS funds for construction of school-cum-cyclone shelters in Orissa.

Defining natural calamity of rare severity as envisaged under para 1.3 of the guidelines on MPLADS.

General:

Since the Member of Parliament Local Area Development Scheme has been framed with the basic objective of giving more opportunity on the part of the Members of Parliament who are the true representatives of the masses to participate directly in the administrative framework of the country, the Department of Statistics and Programme Implementation, Ministry of Planning and Programme Implementation which is the nodal Ministry in respect of the MPLAD scheme needs without debate as per the opinion of the Committee to go into every aspect of short comings inherited in the scheme and remove the same so that a real structural mould could be given to the entire framework of the scheme which could be taken as a true instrument of democratic expression.

Money released under the MPLADS should be deposited in the nationalized banks under a separate account.

Involvement of members with Indira Awaas Yojana projects under MPLADS.

Allocation for each MP under MPLADS should be increased from the present allocation of Rs.1 crore to Rs. 2 crore in view of price rise and shrinkage of value of rupee.

Committee recommended that the work belonging to registered societies and trusts should be permitted under the MPLAD scheme.

Community Centre should be renamed as Common Facilities Centres.

In case of any dispute over the guidelines issued by state government and the guidelines issued by Parliament, latter would prevail.

Inclusion of unaided recognised schools and educational institutions under the ambit of MPLAD scheme.

Guidelines be amended necessarily in the case of retiring members of Rajya Sabha that works recommended by them may be accorded sanction even one day before the retirement of a member.

Shri Oscar Fernandes, MP suggested that there should be separate guidelines for reserving MPLADS funds for the development of weaker sections.

Suggestion regarding review of functioning of MPLADS scheme.

Publicizing list of works under MPLADS by members in leading newspapers.

Waiving the requirement of two years for construction of building rooms for Pandit Sahdev Prasad Mahavidyala, Kanpur.

Award of work to NGOs like BAPS, Swami Narayan and Sewa.

Request for allocation of amount of two crores from MPLADS fund for relief works in Gandhinagar.

List of institutes/projects out of the list furnished by government of Gujarat to be adopted by committee on MPLADS, Rajya Sabha.

Purchase of completed/incompleted Buildings under MPLADS.

Contribute Rs.1.00 crore from MPLADS funds for rehabilitation of the displaced families in Churachandpur district in Manipur.

Removing the cost ceiling of Rs. 25 lakhs per work under MPLADS.

Erection of memorials in the memory of late Sh. G.M.C. Balayogi, ex-speaker, Lok Sabha in Kaikalur, Eluru and Tanuka in Andhra Pradesh.

Hon'ble Deputy Chairman, Rajya Sabha may be allowed to undertake developmental works under MPLADS anywhere in the country, if need be owing to the special position.

Suggestion to amend guidelines on MPLADS for utilization of MPLADS funds for construction of adjacent building near religious places.

Allowing works belonging to registered societies and trusts under MPLADS.

Inclusion of certain works relating to animal care/welfare in the permissible list of works in the guidelines on MPLADS.

Distribution of unspent balances left by the predecessor nominated members of Rajya Sabha among the successor nominated members.

Provision for administrative expenses under MPLADS.

Maintenance of durable assets created in various states out of the MPLADS funds.

Clubbing of funds of more than one M.P. for a single work under one estimate.

Construction of a memorial community hall.

Provision of 50% contribution by state governments to each work taken up under MPLADS.

Ex-Post-Facto approval of Rs. 1.52 crores towards construction of Shri Aurobindo Institute of Indian Culture, Shillong.

Suggestion to amend the guidelines on MPLADS regarding construction of halls or auditoria for the Bar Association of Lawyers outside the state of election of the M.P.

Request from NIF to MPs to allocate MPLADS fund towards scounting, spawning and sustaining grassroot innovations in their constituencies

Request of Shri Narendra Mohan, MP for allocation of amount of two crores from his MPLADS fund for relief works in Gandhinagar.

Revision of Guideline of the MPLADS, Rajya Sabha for utilizing the interest accrued on MPLADS, Rajya Sabha fund.

Contribute Rs.1.00 crore from MPLADS funds for rehabilitation of the displaced families in Churachandpur district in Manipur.

Allow the Deputy Chairman to contribute from her MPLADS fund to the tune of Rs. 83.30 lakhs for the purchase of equipment in the paediatric department of J.J. Hospital, Mumbai.

Clubbing of MPLADS funds in respect of four MPs (3 Rajya Sabha M.Ps and 1 Lok Sabha M.P of Kerala) for the construction of a building for a government college at Chavara, Kerala.

Allot MPLADS Funds to Panchmahal District Cooperative Milk Production Union Ltd.

Treatment of major ailments for people below poverty line.

Inclusion of creation of website in the list of permissible works under the guidelines on MPLADS.

Relaxation for a period of one month for recommending certain changes in the allocation of MPLAD funds after retirement.

6
1001 Ways to Win an Election

The opportunity to spend MPLADS funds is like the sword of Damocles. Voters these days expect MPLADS projects in their locality. If they are not satisfied, their voting behaviour may go against the MP. Of course there are many other factors that influence poll outcome. Thus, as 'election' is central to the MP Funds utilisation, there is a need to find out the determinants of election results and the link between the election and MP Funds utilisation. In this chapter we explore this aspect. However, we deliberately exclude the case of Rajya Sabha MPs as they are elected through a different system.

Determinants of Election Outcomes

There are 1001 ways to win an election and probably, there is equal number of reasons for losing an election. We have randomly selected a few determinants of election outcomes to bring home the fact that the result of an election is influenced by multiple complex factors. The few factors that are explained below are randomly ordered without considering their importance.

Party Manifesto

It is like selling mirror in the kingdom of blinds. In a country of illiterates and semi-literates, party manifestoes are ornamental. These manifestos are solemn pledges to people, agenda in formal written form and are characters of the political parties. These manifestoes are not legally enforceable, though the party in power does not fulfill all the promises. Even the leaders of political parties give little importance to their election manifestos. Morarji Desai, the Prime Minister in 1977, confessed that he had not read the Janata Party Manifesto himself and Rajiv Gandhi, during the 1989 LS election, admitted that "neither anybody reads it nor anyone takes it seriously" (Roy, 2000). But, of late, these manifestos are becoming a sort of witness documents for running coalition governments and opposition. Again, in the age of telecommunication and information, the importance attached to election manifestos is rising. In India, where every vote counts, election manifestos of political parties and coalitions cannot be ignored.

Advertisement

Election campaign through print and electronic media is an integral part in every country. In India, where the government is the largest advertisement spender, the electoral advantage goes to the incumbent government. Campaign films, video CDs, mobile vans equipped with TVs have become very common these days. The impact of advertisement on election outcome is positive but may not be deciding. In this regard, Kalpana Sharma in *The Hindu* asked, "did the electronic media set the agenda or was it led by the more shrewd of the political formations in the country during this (2004) election campaign?" Her answer is "trying to assess whether television coverage of the current elections actually affected opinions or not is virtually impossible". On the other hand many do not support the idea of large spending in advertisement in electronic and print media. "Many politicians and commentators have assented that the lesson to be drawn from the election results is that in future political parties should concentrate on serious issues and avoid consumer-style advertising" (Inden, *The Hindu*, Delhi, 3 Oct., 2004).

Quality format and content of the advertisement also determine its effectiveness in helping the parties. Before 2004 election, the NDA government launched a massive campaign utilising all media. Commenting on this, Ronald B. Inden, professor of history at the University of Chicago, says, "the older governmental ads were informational. The "India Shining" ads were inspirational. They were aimed not at the purely rational citizen who required information in order to make a decision but at people who were also wishers and dreamers. The older ads were also familiar and national. The "India Shining" ads were personal.... urged people to do things themselves" (*The Hindu,* Delhi, 3 Oct., 2004). On the other hand, the Congress Party's ads "Aam Aadmi Ko Kya Mila?" (What did the common man gain?) is remedial in its purpose.

Money Power

Fighting elections with a few lakhs of rupees is unthinkable today. Each candidate is allowed to spend upto Rs.15 lakhs in a parliamentary election under section 77 of the Representation of Peoples Act. But this does not include money spent by the party or the friends. Thus in reality, the real expenditure is nobody's guess.

Commenting on Andhra Pradesh, P. Sainath wrote "a candidate's campaign spending in a single Lok Sabha constituency can be well over Rs.2.5 crores" (P. Sainath, *The Hindu*, Delhi). Though there is no estimate of election expenses in real terms, it differs from constituency to constituency, candidate to candidate and party to party. The probability to win an election improves considerably if the candidates spend a large sum and spend it judiciously.

Communal Politics

In India, every political party follows communal politics, of course, within the electoral democratic framework. Sometimes they gain. Some examples of this type of electoral politics are listed, drawing examples from the 2004 general election:

- Arif Mohammed Khan joined BJP and contested UP's Kaiserganj Lok Sabha seat in 2004. When the BJP was branded a communal party, Khan defended it by commenting on Shri Vajpayee "He is in favour of building bridges with Pakistan and between communities, it is a historic moment and we must grasp it and put an end to the tension between the two communities. This will be an eye opener for everybody, it will prove that fostering good relations between communities is also good politics". But he was proved wrong. Despite the anti-incumbency factor against his rival from SP, Beni Prasad Verma, Khan lost.

- "You look at the 20 important portfolios in the NDA government, is there a single Tamil, Telegu, Malayali, Dalit, Muslim or Christian? This is a government of Hindi-speaking north Indians with a communal agenda, propped up by the RSS", P. Chidambaram tells his constituents. He does not seem to connect commerce and industry among the top 20 portfolios. Both were held by DMK's Murosoli Maran before his death...Muslims and Christians put together are about 13% of the electorate and Chidambaram unfailingly refer to his ally Muslim League in all meetings. Former Congress Rajya Sabha MP Peter Alphonse has been roped in to campaign in Christian dominated areas" (Rajesh Ramachandran, *The Hindu*, Delhi).
- Muslims constitute about 13 per cent of India's population and are in good number in UP, Bihar, West Bengal and J&K and in a few regions of Andhra Pradesh, Karnataka, and Kerala. The community exercises its vote "strategically" in every election based on its concern for individual and community security, educational and economic backwardness and the fear of erosion of their socio-cultural identity. The 'strategic voting' in 2004 elections was to support the candidates who stood the best chance of defeating the BJP. This type of voting behaviour helped the INC, SP, BSP, RJD and the Left parties.
- In Kerala, where electoral results show thin margins, social organisations based on caste, religion and community influence the fate of political parties and candidates by theoretically adopting the strategy of "political equidistance". Nair Service Society, Vishwakarma Sabha, Ezhava Community, Vishala

Catholic Congress are a few communal and caste-based outfits that influence the election outcome by adopting such a strategy.

- Muslims account for about 11 percent of Andhra Pradesh's population and can influence the outcome in 30 to 40 assembly constituencies. Several Muslim social, educational and religion organisations, in a series of pre-2004 election meetings, decided to vote for Congress in LS and TDP in assembly election, reported J.S. Ifthekar in *The Hindu.*
- Eight to nine percent of the population in Maharashtra is Muslims and only in a few places they have large enough concentration – South and South Central Mumbai, Aurangabad and Solapur. Despite the anger with the state government, the community may end up voting for Congress-NCP alliance, writes Kalpana Sharma in *The Hindu* prior to 2004 election. And that is what happened.
- Marathas constitute 29 per cent of voters in Maharashtra, estimated Prafulla Marpakwar in *The Indian Express* and in this context Mahesh Vijapurkar observed in *The Hindu* that "both the NCP-Congress and the Sena-BJP combines are making a strong pitch for the community's vote". Traditionally the Marathas were voting for the Congress but in recent years they are tilted towards Shiv Sena-BJP.

Opinion Polls

"Opinion polls do not threaten but rather fulfill Indian democracy. They provide a forum for ordinary people to interrogate electoral politics. Censoring them would undermine a peoples' democracy" (Rajeev Dhavan, *The Hindu*, Delhi). There is another school that believes that conducting opinion polls and giving them wide publicity may influence voting behaviour. The voters might like to swim along the current (as predicted by the opinion polls) or might even try to invalidate the results. "The Election Commission feared that the prophecies may be self-fulfilling" (Yogesh Atal, *HT*; ND, 22 Sept., 1999). But so long as the reach of the media is limited to only an insignificant segment of the population, publicity of opinion poll results only marginally helps a party or candidate.

Opinion polls in India, so far, are a failure. *India Today*, *Outlook* and *NDTV- The Indian Express* polls on the 2004 general election was based on the views of 17,649, 12,249, and 45,478 voters respectively. For a country of India's size and diversity, such opinion polls to predict election results seem to be irrelevant. Thus the section that believes in the influence of opinion polls on the outcome of elections is grossly mistaken.

Exit Polls

Exit polls in India by market research agencies are invariably done in collaboration with the print and electronic media. The results of such polls are inputs for 24-hours news channels and daily newspapers. Such type of news dissemination may influence the voters, if they go to cast their votes in subsequent time.

"One important argument against publishing the results of exist polls before the last polling booth closes is that such publications interferes with the right of every voter to equal information, and these distort the electoral process" (V.K. Ramachandran, *The Hindu*, Delhi).

Anti-incumbency

Strong anti-incumbency is the hallmark of Indian voters. But anti-incumbency against whom? The sitting MP, the government at New Delhi or the State Government. Most of the times they work hand-in-hand, but when they work in an uncohesive manner, the outcome is mixed. Commenting on 2004 General Election, Commi Kapoor wrote, "The overriding theme of the 2004 Parliamentary Poll results is dissatisfaction with the State Governments and not about who rules New Delhi" (*The Indian Express*, ND). Commenting on the anti-incumbency favour in Jharkhand, Sandeep Dikshit observed in *The Indian Express*, "There is discontentment against the state government, especially due to the bitter infighting among the alliance partners".

Table 6.1
Anti-incumbency against State Government: Party wise Performance

States	*Party in Power*	*No. of Seats*	
		Year: 1999	*Year: 2004*
Karnataka	INC	17	9
Kerala	INC	7	-
Tamil Nadu	AIADMK	11	1
Andhra Pradesh	TDP	29	5
Jharkhand	BJP	11	-
Punjab	INC	8	2
Gujarat	BJP	21	14
Haryana	INLD	5	-
Assam	INC	10	9
Orissa	BJD/BJP	19	19
Uttaranchal	INC	1	1
Himachal Pradesh	BJP	20	22
Chhatisgarh	BJP	8	10
Bihar	RJD	7	20
Rajasthan	BJP	15	20
Maharashtra	INC/NCP	15	20
Uttar Pradesh	SP	27	37
West Bengal	LF	29	35
Delhi	INC	0	6

The ruling parties at the state level improved their tally in Bihar, Delhi, Maharashtra and West Bengal in an impressive manner, though they were in power in the state for many years. In all other states, the ruling party either performed miserably or just maintained its level.

Local Issues

- "Pahle pani, phir Advani"; "Vote Sonia, develop Amethi"; and "Work for me and get my vote", are a few slogans depicting the concerns of the voters on local issues. Commenting on this, Dipankar Gupta wrote, "The 1999 general election turned out to be like municipal election, but held on a national scale. Almost everywhere, local issues counted, even more than local talent. Grand ideological slogans; whether around Kargil, or communalism, made little impact. It is as if voters everywhere decided to nail the lie that politicians can sweet talk their way to power" (Top of the line, *TOI*)

- Sukh Ram won 1996 election from Mandi despite his involvement in the telecom scam. Kalpanath Rai won 1996 election from Ghosi despite being in jail. It is understood that both of them impressively worked for the development of their constituencies.
- Poppy cultivation in Chuhar valley at the Mandi LS constituency (Himachal Pradesh) was an election issue in 2004, like in the earlier election. Both the BJP and the Congress promised to legalise poppy cultivation. An estimated 20,000 families are dependent on this activity (Maheshwar Singh of BJP lost to Pratibha Singh).
- Pune experienced a demographic change due to industrial growth and expansion of new business opportunities. Though Suresh Kalmadi (Congress) is not exactly popular with the powerful Maratha community, he won.
- Akbarpur in UP is the constituency of BSP supremo Mayawati. A 300-bed hospital, city flyovers and district status to Akbarpur sanctioned by Mayawati were cancelled by the next CM, Mulayam Singh Yadav. This became a local issue in 2004 election. Mayawati played the usual victim-card and won the election.
- CPI(M)'s V. P. Kulkarni fought with issues of irrigation, debt burden on peasantry and farm power tariff in Belgaum constituency in Karnataka and lost the election to Angadi Suresh Chanabasappa of BJP.
- Gobichettipalayam in Tamil Nadu is known as an AIDMK fortress (1980, 1984, 1989, 1991, 1998 and 1999 election). Water became the prime issue as the whole area reeled under a drought and farmers were unable to cultivate paddy or cash crops. The vulnerability of cultivation went up due to dwindling water storage level in the Bhavanisagar dam to 1.5 tmc ft. as against its capacity

of 32.8 tmc ft. Other issues were central value added tax that was supposed to add to the woes of the weavers and the non-implementation of the decades-old Palani-Chamrajnagar rail project. E.V.K S. Elangovan of INC exploited these issues to his advantage and won the 2004 election.

- Leh region of Ladakh constituency in Jammu and Kashmir is predominantly Buddhist, but Muslims dominate Kargil. The issue of granting Union Territory or Hill Council status has played an important role in all the recent elections there.
- Coimbatore in Tamil Nadu is famous as the "Manchester of the East". CPI candidate K. Subbarayan's strategy revolved around the problem of industrial sickness and closure and the central value added tax. He defeated the BJP candidate who had won the last two elections.
- Individual, family and community security has always been the concern of the people of Udhampur parliamentary constituency in Kashmir. The BJP won here in 1996, 1998 and 1999 elections. "In the 1996... the BJP contested on the slogan of handing over Doda district to the Army. It got the bulk of the Hindu votes – approximately 70 percent - and the victory was made smooth by the Muslim boycott... But things have changed lately. A sense of security has been restored in the area, particularly during the 2002 Assembly election" (Luv Puri, *The Hindu*, Delhi). Chaman Lal Gupta of the BJP lost to Lal Singh of INC in the 2004 election.
- In Dahanu in Maharashtra, farmers - mostly fruit cultivators, demanded that the coal-based 500 MW power plant of Reliance Energy should switch to a cleaner fuel such as natural gas. Meena Menon of *The Indian Express* reported the view of the BJP sitting MP and 2004 candidate, Chintamani Wanaga – "There must be some technical evidence to prove the power plant is causing pollution. Only then can we demand it shut down". He lost the election to the INC candidate.

- Acute drinking water scarcity and problem in undertaking normal farming activities are the outcome of lesser release of water by the Karnataka in the Cauvery delta districts of Tamil Nadu. This became the only major issue in the Thanjavur, Mayileduturai and Nagapattinam constituencies. Though local people blamed the Congress ruled State of Karnataka for their misery, they voted the same party and its alliance DMK in all the three districts.
- Express News Service examined the pre-election mood in the drought-affected districts of Maharashtra and reported that all the work on the various water projects taken up by the Krishna Valley Development Corporation in the region is at a standstill because of lack of funds. The voters are angry with sitting MPs Prakashbapu Patil of Sangli, Laxman Patil of Satara and Ramdas Athavle of Pandharpur, who have not even visited the area. All the three are in fray again, but party workers are reluctant to campaign in drought zone. "We have no answer to offer to the affected people", they admit. All three retained their seats.
- Revocation of the Armed Forces Special Powers Act was the main issue during the 2004 election and was supported by political parties of all hues. This issue gained importance in Manipur having two LS constituencies.
- In Kerala, the fishing community has an influential presence in 13 out of 20 Lok Sabha constituencies. Foreign trawlers and globalisation of Indian seas are local issues that determine the voting behaviour of this community.
- Floods are a perennial poll issue in West Bengal's Raiganj LS constituency and cheap Chinese yarn a big issue during polls in Varanasi in Uttar Pradesh. The city is home to the three lakh strong Momin or Ansari community.

All these examples drawn from the recent LS election are only indicative. There is every possibilities that local issues may confuse the jurisdictions of elected representatives.

Poll Alliances (local, state and national)

The Congress days of Pandit Nehru and Indira Gandhi are history now. Coalition governments have been a reality since early 1990s. All sorts of regional and sub-regional parties are playing a crucial role in winning elections. Pre-poll alliances are becoming powerful enough to determine election results.

- Ladakh: In 2004 polls, the Congress, which has full control over the Leh Autonomous Hill Development Council, backed an independent candidate – Thupstan Chhewang. The National Conference candidates who won in 1998 and 1999 were defeated by Chhewang.
- Maneka Gandhi won UP's Pilibhit seat in 2004 and 1999, as an independent candidate. Her opponent V.M. Singh seemed to have won over the minority Muslims as he took up the TADA cases as a lawyer; but she won due to alliance with BJP.
- In 1999 LS election, P. Chidambaram fought without allies and lost. But in 2004, he not only got Congress ticket but also the Congress constituency, Sivaganga (TN) and the support of DMK, MDMK and the Communists. He won.
- Due to pre-poll alliances, the BJP and INLD combinely won 10 LS seats in 1999. But by the time of the next general elections in 2004, that had become history and both fielded candidates in each constituency of Haryana. Anti-incumbency and poll-alliance factors resulted in electoral flip-flop – except the Sonepat seat, which was won by the BJP, all went to INC and HVC.
- Wilfred D'Souza of NCP lost the 2004 election to Shripad Y. Naik of BJP in Panaji though the NCP and Congress had a poll-alliance and all the seven Congress MLAs of the 18 assembly constituencies in Panaji had extended support to him.
- The Telengana Rastra Samiti (TRS) demanded separate statehood for Telengana and became a force just before the 2004 general election. The Congress forged an alliance with TRS and won most of the assembly as well

as Lok Sabha constituencies (the tally improved from 5 in 13th LS to 29 in 14th LS). It also gained from its alliance with CPI and the CPM.

- "The return to power of Mulayam Singh Yadav and the new compulsion of Western Uttar Pradesh's electoral politics have led Ajit Singh's RLD to ally with the Samajwadi Party", wrote Venkitesh Ramakrishnan in *The Hindu*. This alliance worked and the RLD-SP candidates won in Muzaffarnagar, Kairana and Saharanpur and lost only the Meerut constituency in Western UP in 2004.
- "The BJP's emergence as the frontrunner in Karnataka owes to the crucial alliance it forged with the Janta Dal (U)", wrote Parvathi Menon in *The Hindu*. "Though a junior partner in the alliance, the JD (U) has provided the BJP access to social classes and castes that the party could not have otherwise hoped for."
- The MY (Muslim and Yadavs) factor helped Laloo Prasad Yadav's Rashtriya Janata Dal to garner 28.3 percent of votes in 1999 LS election, though it suffered defeat in the hands of the BJP, the Janta Dal (United) and the Samta Party. But in 2004 LS election, Ram Vilas Paswan (LJP) left NDA and joined RJD-Congress, NCP and CPI(M) combined. This coalition gained the votes of Muslims, Yadavs and dalits and resulted in the increase in seats for all these parties (INC from 2 to 3, RJD from 7 to 20 and LJP/CPM from 4 to 6).

Single Event

There are many instances where election results are predictably dependent on solo events. In most of the cases, these are emotional issues. Some recent examples:

- Madhavarao Scindia's unfortunate death in an air crash prompted his son Jyotiraditya Scindia to contest the Guna LS seat in February 2002, which he won. The sympathy wave gave him a hefty lead of more than 4.5 lakh votes.

- BJP won 10 out of 12 Parliamentary constituencies in 2004 LS election in Chhatisgarh. But Ajit Jogi the former CM and INC candidate could win the Mahasamund constituency as he met with a serious accident and was undergoing treatment at a Mumbai hospital during the campaign time. Sonia Gandhi ensured his arch rival Digvijay Singh, Ashok Gehlot, Moti Lal Vora and others visit Mahasamund and campaigned for Jogi. "Even Atal Bihari Vajpayee, the PM said to have refused to address a rally in Mahasamund while the rival candidate lay in hospital" (Aarti Dhar, *The Hindu*, Delhi).

Caste

- Even before independence, caste politics existed in India. This got strength under the constitutional provisions of reservation of LS and assembly seats for the scheduled castes. The caste factor became a real force under various dalit parties of Maharashtra and BSP, SP, RJD, etc, under the headship of Kansi Ram, Mayawati, Lalu Prasad Yadav and Mulayam Singh Yadav, to name a few.
- "Sack Rabri, jail Lalu and save the Kurmis from the Yadavs" was a slogan in Bihar election by Samata Party. Madhepura in Bihar has an estimated 30 per cent Yadav voters. It became the battle ground for two Yadav chieftains – Lalu Prasad and Sharad Yadav. Some of Medhepura's influential Rajputs, who supported Sharad Yadav in 1999 election, have joined Lalu Prasad in 2004 election.
- Commenting on 2004 polls in Chhapra in Bihar, Vinay Kumar wrote in *The Hindu* "The local caste equations are discussed threadbare whenever people gather to talk about elections. The dominant castes here are the Rajputs (3 lakh) and the Yadavs (3.5 lakh). There are also 2 lakh dalits, 1.25 lakh upper castes, 80,000 Muslims and 80,000 Kurmis. Clearly, Mr. Rudy is banking upon the Rajputs, the upper caste and the Kurmis and hoping for a division in the Muslim and Yadav votes". Re-polling was done after Election Commission discovered incidents

of violence during the poll. Laloo Prasad Yadav, the RJD President and former CM won. As a professor of local college observed earlier- "It will be an interesting electoral tussle to watch. You may find Yadavs working for Mr. Rudy and Rajputs working for Mr. Yadav."

- In 1999 elections, Ram Vilas Paswan won in the Hajipur constituency in Bihar with the support of Kurmis, Thakurs, Bhumihars and Brahmins, who add up to estimated 20 per cent of the votes. He was with the NDA. But in 2004, he was not with the NDA and relied on support of Yadavs and Muslims, who constitute about 22 percent of the voters. But he again won as the Dussadhs, to which he belongs and who comprise 12 percent of the voters balanced the number in his favour.
- Shanta Kumar, though a political heavyweight, lost the 2004 election in Kangra in Himachal Pradesh, his home ground. The Congress nominated a "Girth"(scheduled caste) community candidate, Chander Kumar, and the support of Rajputs was assured by CM Virbhadra Singh. Besides factionalism with the BJP, the Rajput-Girth combination became formidable for Shanta Kumar in Kangra district, where his Brahmin community comprises only about 20 per cent of the voters.
- Even though caste considerations are a major factor while voting, this issue is never raised during election campaign – not even in the SC-reserved seats. This was observed in Tonk in Rajasthan, a seat reserved for SCs, where mostly power and water shortage issues were raised, but not related to dalits.
- "Caste considerations will be decisive here," wrote Anita Jashua, in *The Hindu* for Sultanpur in UP. Of the total voter thirteen per cent are Muslims, 26 per cent scheduled castes and 14 percent Brahmins. A Muslim revealed the 2004 caste factor to Anita Jashus as saying "if the Brahmins decide to vote for the BJP, then Muslims may go with Tahir (BSP candidate), but if the Brahmins shift to Congress, Muslims are likely to vote for Captain

Sharma (INC candidate and Gandhi family loyalist)". Mohammad Tahir of BSP won.

- BJP also relies on the caste factor to gain in electoral politics. It they re-admitted Kalyan Singh and hoped to influence voting pattern in Lodh heartland of Uttar Pradesh.

POTA Poltics

Harassing political opponents is common. This becomes easier when the ruling party has with them an instrument like POTA (Prevention of Terrorism Act) in its hand. The opposition also never forgets to use the same to blame the ruling party for misuse of POTA. This refers to POTA politics, which also influences election results.

- Raghuraj Pratap Singh, better known as "Raja Bhaiya" of Pratapgarh in UP was booked under POTA by Mayawati government. He claims, as "an independent MLA, I had the courage to ask her to prove her majority on the floor of the House. It was a democratic demand but soon after that cases were registered against me and my father".
- Kalpana Sharma observed that prior to the 2004 polls, "the use of POTA has alienated Muslims in villages across Maharashtra; this could rebound on the Congress-NCP alliance" – the ruling coalition that has the authority to invoke POTA.
- Tamil Nadu case: Jayalalitha of AIADMK booked Vaiko, leader of Marumalarchi Dravida Munnetra Kazhagam (MDMK), under POTA in July 2002 and kept him in custody for 18 months. This issue was made a major poll-campaigning instrument by the DMK and its allies in TN during the 2004 election. The misuse of POTA by Jayalalitha was one of the reasons behind the parting of ways between the BLP and the DMK.

Pre-Poll Bonanza

Providing a number of bonanzas prior to election is popular with ruling parties. It is assumed that such bonanzas would draw more votes.

Maithili language was included in the Eighth Schedule of the Constitution prior to 2004 general election. It was expected to benefit the NDA as it was claimed that the language is spoken in 14 parliamentary constituencies in the Bihar.

Scheduled tribes (STs) can influence the election outcome in as many as 100 constituencies, besides the reserved one. As a pre-poll bonanza, the NDA government issued an official order in February to regularise the tribal rights on forestland for encroachments upto 1993. This cut-off year was 1980 till then. The Forest (Conservation) Act was diluted further and more power was granted to the state governments allowing them to decide on forest clearance for developmental projects.

The People's Democratic Party-led coalition government in Jammu & Kashmir recommended in February 2004 that those who speak the Pahari language be included in the official list of scheduled tribes in spite of language not being a criteria for identifying scheduled tribe.

Dynasties

Winning elections easily by the members of political and ruling dynasties is common in India. A few cases are cited below:

- Dushyant Singh, 31, a scion of the Dholpur royal family in Rajasthan is linked to the Scindia royal family from his mother's side. He contested from Jhalawar, the constituency represented by his mother Vasundhera Raje till she became the CM of Rajasthan and won the 2004 election.
- Jyotiraditya Scindia, son of late Madhavrao Scindia and grand-son of Vijayaraje Scindia, is from the royal family of Gwalior. He became the youngest MP in 2002 when he won the Guna seat after the death of his father.
- Dayanidhi Maran, son of DMK leader Murasoli Maran, contested the Central Chennai constituency in 2004 and won it at the age of 37. His father was dead by then.
- Rahul Gandhi, the scion of the Nehru-Gandhi family, once said, "My father is my hero; I am my father's son, why should I mind if people see him in me?" He won the

Amethi constituency in UP in his maiden attempt in 2004.

- Milind Deora, the 27-years old son of veteran Congress leader Murli Deora, won from Mumbai South in 2004 general election. His father represented the same constituency from 1984 to 1996 and again for 13 months in 1998-99.
- O.P. Chautala's son, Ajay, Bansilal's son, Surender and Shamsher Singh and Surjewala's son, Randeep lost the 2004 general election in Haryana.

Foreign Origin

Sharad Pawar and Purna Sangma of NCP made an issue out of Sonia Gandhi's foreign origin in 1999 election. During 2004 election, the former reconciled and made an alliance with INC in Maharashtra. On the other hand despite BJP's harping on the Congress president's place of birth as a major issue in the run-up to the 2004 polls, the outcome was not encouraging for BJP. In Uttar Pradesh, some believe a woman does not have her own caste but takes the caste of her father and then of the man she marries. So there is no question of Sonia being a foreigner after marriage. The issue of foreign origin of the leader of a political party does influence a section of the voters for not supporting the party.

Dalit Power

The constitution of India classified the downtrodden as scheduled caste. The political and social movement started by Jotiba Phule and Dr. B.R. Ambedkar unified them under 'Dalit' category and Kansi Ram and Mayawati turned them into vote banks. Traditionally, the SCs/Dalits were voted for the Congress but in recent years, many of them have shifted there loyalities to the Bahujan Samaj Party in the Ganga plains, Dravidian parties in the south and clone dalit partiies in Maharashtra. The Republican Party of India (RPI) was established by Dr. B.R. Ambedkar in early 1950s. The Dalit Panthers of India of early 1970s and Bahujan Samaj Party of the 1980s are political forces of considerable significance.

The dalits primarily, a fraction of RPI, moved closer to Shiv Sena, a regional party in recent years. This was visible from slogans like "Shiv-Bhim Shakti".

BSP fielded 435 candidates across 25 states and UTs in the 2004 LS election, much more than the national parties like the Congress and the BJP. Its sole share increased from 4.16 per cent in the 1991 general election to 11.21 per cent in 1996.

Muscle, Mafia and Arms

"Despite serious efforts made by the Election Commission to decriminalise politics, candidates with criminal backgrounds have come to dominate most regions of Uttar Pradesh in the run-up to the Lok Sabha election", wrote J.P. Sukla in the *Indian Express*. The reasoning behind their (candidates having criminal records) nominations appears to be that they have the muscle power to win, this more than anything else decided in their facour". Bihar is not far behind in this regard. Intimidating voters through fear-tactics to gain votes in elections occurs in all parts of India. It is true of Naxlite affected areas of Andhra Pradesh, Orissa, Jharkhand and Chhatisgarh.

Vote Split

Political parties and candidate take special care to split the opponents vote banks. Small regional parties and local leaders are used for this. Instigating dummy candidates to contest election is common. For example, before 1996 elections, Congress had won the Solarpur constituency in Maharashtra eight times, but it lost to the BJP because 1.66 lakh anti-BJP voters went to the Janta Dal nominee.

Election Schedule: Length and Spacing

Money, manpower and material are used by political parties and candidates according to their strategy. As these resources are limited, their utilization over time plays a crucial role. Thus, election schedule assumes importance for determining the election result. The Election Commission, Home Ministry and the government may have their logistics problem in mind while drawing the election schedule but political parties take it seriously

Table 6.2
Election Schedule in 1999 and 2004 Lok Sabha Election

	1999 election			*2004 election*		
	Seats	*Date*	*Gaps with preceding poll day*	*Seats*	*Date*	*Gaps with preceding poll day*
Phase 1	145	Sept. 4	-	141	April 20	-
Phase II	124	Sept.11	6 days	137	April 26	6 days
Phase III	78	Sept 18	6 days	83	May 5	9 days
Phase IV	74	Sept 25	6 days	182	May 10	5 days
Phase V	119	Oct 3	8 days	-	-	-

as it influences their campaign plan. Election to the Eleventh and Twelve Lok Sabha were conducted in four days, while for 1999 election, it was done in as many as 26 days.

On 1999 general election, Meenu Roy commented that "the unprecedented decision to stretch the polls for a month, from September 4 to October 3, led to a ludicrous situation where a national election had reduced to the level of a local election. It was interesting that while Delhi was ready to vote, candidates in Calcutta did not even file their nominations. So it was impossible for anybody, including political parties to get a clear cross country picture" (Roy, 2000: 240). The polling to 14th LS continued from April 20 to May 10 - a total of 21 days. Under such a situation resourceful parties have an advantage.

Pre-Poll Promises

Muslim Muttahida Mahaz of Andhra Pradesh was given an assurance by N. Chandrababu Naidu, the CM prior to 2004 election that Muslims would be given three per cent reservation in all walks of life. The Congress promised free power to farmers and to 'single-bulb households' in Andhra Pradesh before 2004 election.

Such promises are a sort of trap. Their effectiveness is diminishing as Indian matures.

War

War, whether won or lost, is always an election issue. It is true for the United States (Korean War, Missile Crisis 1960,

Vietnam, Gulf war 1991, Iraq 2003), United Kingdom (World War I and II) and all other countries including India (1962 China war, 1965 Indo-Pak war, 1971 liberation of Bangladesh). Commenting on Iraq war, historian Eric Hobsbawn said "The terms 'War Against Terrorism' is not possible. It is nothing but a piece of rhetoric. It is not an efficient way of fighting. For both America and Britain, it is more a method of mobilising and de-mobilising their domestic constituency" *(The Hindu, Delhi,* 22 Dec., 2004*)*. The undeclared war of Kargil was a major issue in the 1999 Lok Sabha election. Meenu Roy observed "The Kargil war was fought in and for Kashmir and it was the greatest election theme elsewhere in the country, but in the valley, however, it was a non-issue....This was clearly no Kargil election, as the results in the battle ground states of Uttar Pradesh and Punjab underlined. Further, the Kargil effect was in visible decline during the later part of election" (Roy, 2000: 83 and 249). Thus, a war may influence the national psychie in general, but locally it may not be forceful enough to give electoral advantage.

Vajpayee Factor

At times, an Indian election resembles the presidental election of the United States – "Bush versus Kerry", "Vajpayee versus Sonia". Atal Bihari Vajpayee became a 'national phenomenon' during his 13-days rule and 13-months rule. This gave the NDA some advantage during the 1999 general election. But in 2004 election, though Vajpayee was standing tall, he was physically weak. Not much dividend was gained from a "tried, tested, trusted" leadership. "Along the Golden Quadrilateral, its Vajapee all the way" said Harish Khare in *The Hindu* with regard to Karnataka. And, "in contrast to Karnataka, there are obvious limits to Atal Bihari Vajpayee's image and popularity in Andhra Pradesh", Khare wrote.

Charisma and Personality

A few days before 2004 election, 22 people were killed in a stampede during a sari distribution function organised on the birthday celebration of a BJP functionary in Lucknow, the LS constituency of Vajpayee. This became a front page story in newspapers, all electronic media covered it with enthusiasm, and a first information report was filled after the Election Commission issued an adverse order. Even eminent lawyer Ram Jethmalani took it up vigorously in his campaign. Despite all this, Vajpayee won the election.

Film actor Govinda (INC) defeated Ram Naik (BJP) in Mumbai North in 2004 election with the yell of people "Govinda Ala Re". Ram Naik, a five times MP from Mumbai North and a cabinet minister in the NDA the government could not stand in front of the new comer.

Till 1996, the Congress had won eight times in Solapur in Maharashtra. In 1998 election, it brought Sushil Kumar Shinde, then a RS MP and a dalit, to fight the BJP. Shinde recaptured the constituency in 1998 and repeated the feat in 1999. But when Shinde became the CM and somebody else contested the 2004 election, the BJP won.

Haren Pandya, the former Gujarat Home Minister, was shot dead in March 2003 while he was taking his morning walk at Ahmedabad's Law Garden. His father Vithalbhai Pandya contested the 2004 election against L.K. Advani, as he could not get justice from senior BJP leaders. The latter was then the Deputy. PM. Advani's charisma worked and Vithalbhai Pandya was defeated with a large margin. The unfavourable caste equations and dissatisfaction among government servants (especially the Diwali bonus issue) could not stop Advani from winning.

A.B.A. Ghani Khan Choudhary entered the LS for eighth time from Malda in West Bengal. Better known as "Barkat-da" to party workers and "Babu-mian" to his community, he has always been a winning card for the Congress. Trinamul Congress had eight out of 42 seats in the 13th LS, but, barring Mamta Banerjee, all lost.

The 14th LS is represented by 62 MPs, who have won for five times and more. They are charismatic and due to their personality, are elected repeatedly. Their chances of winning an election are high. Name of such leaders are given in Table 6.3.

Table 6.3
Tall and Popular Leaders

Number of LS election won	*14th Lok Sabha Members (Party- no. of times)*
10 times or more	Somnath Chatterjee (CPM)
Seven to Nine times	Basudeb Acharia (CPM-8), Anil Basu (CPM-7), Chandra Shekhar (SJPCR-8), A. B. A Ghanikhan Choudhury (INC-8), Santosh Mohan Dev (INC-7), Giridhar Gamang (INC-8), MN Gavit (INC-8), Satyanarayan Jatiya (BJP-7), Kamal Nath (INC-7), Sanat Kumar Mandal (RSP-8), Hannan Mallah (CPM-8), Rupchand Pal (CPM-7), Laxinarayan Pandey (BJP-7), Ram Vilas Paswan (LJSP-7), Balasaheb Vikhe Patil (SS-8), Ram Chandra Veerappa (BJP-7), Purna Agitok Sangma (NCP-8), Manabendra Shah (BJP-8), Atal Bihari Vajpayee (BJP-8), George Fernandes (Samta Party-8), Anil Basu (CPM-7),
Five to Six times	Lal Krishna Advani (BJP-5), E. Ahmed (MLKSC-5), Ramesh Bais (BJP-5), Mamta Kumari Banerjee (AITC-6), Girdhari Lal Bhargav (BJP-6), P. Chidambaram (INC-6), Shivraj Singh Chouhan (BJP-5), Priya Ranjan Dasmunshi (INC-5), Mohanbhai Delkar (Ind.-5), Ram Chandra Dome (CPM-6),Sunil Dutt (INC-5), Maneka Gandhi (Ind-5), Santosh Kumar Gangwar (BJP-5), Bijay Kishna Handique (INC-5), Ramkrishna Kusmaria (BJP-5), Sumitra Mahajan (BJP-6), Bir Singh Mahato (FBL-5), K.N. Muniyappa (INC-5), Rupchand Murmu (CPM-5), Vilas Baburao Mittemwar (INC -5), Nitish Kumar (Samta Party -5), Sukdeo Paswan (RJDP-5), Harin Pathak (BJP-5), Prakash V. Patil (INC-50), Sharad C.G. Powar (NCP-6), Kashi Ram Rana (BJP-6), Naranbhai J. Rathawa (INC-5), Mohan Rawala (SS-5), Rasa Singh Rawat (BJP-5), Baju Ban Riyan (CPM-6), Arjun Charan Sethi (BJP-6), Saleem Iqbal Shervani (SP-5), Ajit Singh (RLD-5), Lakshman Singh (INC-5), Shibu Soren (JMM-6), P.C. Thomas (IFDP-6), Tarit Baran Topdar (CPM-6), Shanker Sinh Vaghela (INC-5), Ratilal Kalidas Varma (BJP-6), Devendra Prasad Yadav (JDU-5).

Table 6.4
Political Parties in General Elections

		1998	1999	2004
1.	Nos. of Parties	176	169	230
2.	Nos. of Parties not winning even a single seat	137	131	177
3.	Nos. of Parties winning only one seat	12	13	12
4.	Nos. of Parties winning more than 1% of votes	16	15	16

No-Show Parties

Some of the candidates are sure of their defeat, but still they get a party nomination to fight an election. They get financial help to contest and divide the voters. Such parties and their candidates at times influence poll results in a significant manner. The absurdity of such parties is clear from the table above:

Voter Apathy

Low turnout of voters helps a few candidates to win easily. Frequent elections, long election periods and political instability contributes to voter apathy. The middle class has become disenchanted with the democratic process as they cannot identify themselves with any issue or political party.

Table 6.5
Lok Sabha Election Duration and Voter Turnout

Year	*Duration of Election*	*Voter Turnout (in %)*	*Urbanized States*
1991	26 days	55.88	53.25
1996	11 days	57.94	54.87
1998	13 days	62.00	58.96
1999	29 days	60.00	58.21
2004		58.07	56.28

Voter apathy is observed among privileged citizens as change of governments hardly matters to them. The unprivileged citizens too do not want to vote, as they perceive no change in their living conditions, in spite of change in power. A large section also does not vote as it thinks the candidates are either useless or harmful. "Unkept promises of politicians kept voters away more than anything else. Anantnag parliamentary constituency recorded the lowest of 16 per cent polling. The ruling PDP, during 2002 assembly polls, had promised one job to every family besides promising to disband the special task force of J & K police and providing good governance" (M. Saleem Pandit, *TIE*, ND).

Postal and Proxy Vote

Postal and Proxy vote is allowed under Representatives of People Act. During 2004 general election 6,05,434 postal votes and 532 proxy votes were cast. Postal and proxy votes comprise 0.4 per cent of total votes in West Bengal, and 0.3 per cent in Rajasthan and Tamil Nadu. Though small in number, they have a bearing on election results.

Electronic Voting

The conventional ballot box and ballot papers method was subject to manipulation and rigging. This is countered to a large extent with the introduction of the electronic voting machines (EVMs). This simple-to-operate machine changed the electoral procedure by making the process easier and faster. For the first time, the 1999 Lok Sabha polls used EVMs in 46 constituencies, though these were experimentally introduced in 1983 elections in a few places. Scope of misuse or unsuitability of EVMs cannot be ignored. Satinath Choudhary, a former professor of computer science and the president of Better Democracy Forum, the Bronx, New York, has warned about the theoretical possibility to replace original EVMs with doctored ones. Bunker Ray of Barefoot College, Rajasthan has great reservation on use of EVMs. According to him, "the state polls were deeply flawed by EVMs. In numerous villages, voters who lined-up for hours never actually voted. The button was pressed on their behalf".

TINA Factor

In past elections, especially during Pandit Nehru and Indira Gandhi, the impression that there is no alternative (TINA) to congress and so, votes should not be wasted by supporting others, played a crucial role.

Stability

Government's stability is a precondition for ensuring good governance and delivery of pre-poll promises. Vajpayee's 13-day and 13-month rule brought the stability issue to the forefront. The NDA government even wanted a constitutional amendment to establish the government for a full five-year term in the name of stability. On the other hand, for BSP, instability is a tool to break the hegemony of the upper caste parties like the NDA and the Congress. Stability plank for the Congress gave rise to the slogan: "In independent India, Congress gave five PMs in fifty two years but in five years the non-congress parties gave seven PMs." The scene was no different during the 2004 general election. "Very early in the campaign, it became obvious that the 'India shining' propaganda was the biggest self-goal of the 14th Lok Sabha elections. The BJP changed track mid-way and has since been campaigning on the platform of stability" (C. Rammanohar Ray, *The Indian Express,* Delhi).

Sarpanch (head of village panchayat)

Sarpanchs are the village Panchayat heads elected through popular universal franchise under the provisions of 73rd Constitutional Amendments. They have a big role to play in all elections. "110 km. from Mumbai, a tribal hamlet votes only because the local sarpanch tells them to," reported Shailesh Gaikwad in *The Indian Express.*

"Threatening village sarpanches with dismissal" by the state government is an instrument of wooing voter. In Khajuraho Lok Sabha constituency, "of the 130 sarpanches in the district, alleges the Congress, 110 have been threatened with dismissal" (*Indian Express*, ND, 5 May, 2004).

Preceding Assembly and Local Elections

Election strategies are designed according to assembly, block and village levels. At times, it is carried up to the polling booth level. Election performances of the preceding elections are studied to design strategies for the next.

Sagar in Madhya Pradesh has eight assembly segments. The BJP won in seven segments in assembly polls and the Congress got its lone victory in Surkhi. Virendra Kumar of BJP won the 2004 election.

The BJP lost all the five Assembly segments in Lakhimpur Kheri in UP in 2002. Even though the BJP filled Vinay Katiyar, BJP's state president and the icon of a pan-Hindu social identity, the 2004 election result could not be reversed. This is despite the fact that Lakhimpur Kheri was electing only a Kurmi leader since 1952 and Katiyar is a Kurmi.

Table 6.6
2003 and 2002 Assembly Election Result Party-wise

2003 Assembly Elections				*2002 Assembly Elections*			
State	*Party*	*No. of Seats*		*State*	*Party*	*No. of Seats*	
		Contested	*Won*			*Contested*	*Won*
Chhatisgarh (LS seats–11)	BJP	90	50	Uttar Pradesh (LS seats – 80)	BJP	320	88
	BSP	54	02		BSP	401	98
	INC	90	37		CPM	06	02
	NCP	89	01		INC	402	25
Madhya Pradesh (LS seats–29)	BJP	230	173		SP	390	143
	BSP	157	02	Uttaranchal (LS seats – 5)	BJP	69	19
	CPM	09	01		BSP	68	07
	INC	229	38		INC	70	36
	NCP	105	01		NCP	26	01
	JD(U)	36	01		OTH	-	07
	SP	161	07	Goa (LS seats – 2)	BJP	39	17
	OTH	-	4		INC	40	16
Rajasthan (LS seats–25)	BJP	197	120		NCP	20	01
	BSP	124	04		OTH	-	06
	CPM	18	01	Gujarat (LS seats - 26)	BJP	182	127
	INC	200	56		INC	180	51
	OTH	-	21		JD(U)	29	02
Delhi (LS seats–7)	BJP	70	20		OTH	-	02
	INC	70	47	J & K (LS seats – 06)	INC	78	20
	NCP	33	01		JKNC	85	28
	OTHERS	-	02		PDP	59	16
Himachal Pradesh (LS seats–04)	BJP	68	16		OTH	-	23
	INC	68	43	Manipur (LS seats – 02)	BJP	46	04
	HVC	49	01		CPI	16	05
	OTH	-	02		INC	58	20
Meghalaya (LS seats–2)	BJP	28	02		NCP	33	03
	INC	60	22		FPM	48	13
	NCP	54	14		MPP	14	02
	OTH	-	22		MSCP	42	07
Mizoram (LS seat – 01)	INC	40	12		SAP	31	03
	MNF	39	21	Punjab (LS seats – 13)	BJP	23	03
	OTH	-	07		INC	105	62
Nagaland (LS seats–01)	BJP	38	07		SAD	92	41
	NC	60	21		OTH	-	09
	JD(U)	13	03				
	OTH	-	10				
Tripura (LS seats–02)	CPM	55	38				
	INC	42	13				
	OTH	-	08				

Results of the preceding elections to the state assemblies and panchayati raj institutions influence the results of the general Lok Sabha election. At the national level, the ruling party's calculations based on the last election prompts it to choose the election timings. The NDA (especially BJP) government based on the performances in the assembly elections held in 2003 in Madhya Pradesh, Rajasthan and Chhatisgarh and earlier in 2002 in Gujarat dissolved the house (LS) and opted for an early poll. This calculated risk failed to give sufficient dividend to the BJP and the NDA.

Outsider-Insider

Voters judge a candidate from many angles. A local candidate is mostly favoured over an outsider. But there are scores of examples where the voters ignore the outsider issue.

Jayaprada won Rampur LS seat in Uttar Pradesh in 2004 as a SP candidate though she is from Andhra Pradesh. Probably SP's Muslim vote bank supported her as she left TDP as the later's silence on the Gujarat riot. Navjot Singh Sidhu (BJP) belongs to Patiala but won the 2004 election from Amritsar. Vinay Katiyar (BJP) shifted to Lakhimpur Kheri (UP) to get the support of the Kurmi community, but lost in 2004.

Parliament Performance

The voters are increasingly judging their MP performance in the Parliament in recent years. Thanks to the live telecast of the proceedings of the houses and wide coverage in the print media, educated and sensitive voters have started watching their MPs closely.

Six-time MP Uttamrao Deorao Patil who has won all the six contests since 1980, lost the 2004 election despite the Congress-NCP pact. Probably his parliamentary performance was the main factor. The public "seem to know about him is his getting caught 'napping' in Parliament a few years ago" (Vivek Despande, *The Indian Express, ND*).

Bijli, Sadak and Pani (electricity, roads and water)

Common man well-being is always an election issue in a democracy. *Roti-kapda-makan*, *bijli-sadak-pani* and *jal-jangal-zameen* are the basis of human survival and till today Indians are struggling to get these.

BJP won the assembly elections in Madhya Pradesh, Rajasthan and Chhattisgarh in 2003 and interpreted it as vote against the state governments as the later failed to meet the basic needs of citizens. They got carried away by the macro economic achievements in terms of growth rates and thought that it will help all sections and regions. They went wrong and lost the 2004 elections.

Separate State

The issue of statehood for the Vidarbha region of Maharashtra is always an election issue but could not gain ground due to the stand taken by major political parties. Like Telengana, it could not get an effective leadership or regional party. Thus the influence of this issue became weak, while in AP, the Telengana issue paid rich dividend to INC and TRS alliance. Writing in *The Hindu*, K. Venkateshwaralu said, "the separatist sentiment in this [Telengana] region of Andhra Pradesh is so strange that political parties have been forced to re-engineer their poll strategies." Even Congress conceded 42 Assembly seats and 6 LS seats to K. Chandrasekhar Rao's Telengana Rashtra Samiti in 2004 election. The INC-TRS alliance got landslide victory in Andhra Pradesh, both in the assembly as well as Parliament elections.

Factional Politics

Factionalism is common in a competitive electoral politics. Each and every party are subjected to factional politics in a dynamic political party system. This phenomenon also influences the election result.

Factionalism in Congress is not new in Kerala but it reached its zenith in 2004 between A.K. Antony and K. Karunakaran. INC, which was holding 7 LS seats in 13th Lok Sabha, could not manage even a single seat in the 14th Lok Sabha.

Rajas and Nawabs

The rajas, maharajas, nawabs and clan chieftains are influential people and are in a position to influence the electoral politics either directly or indirectly. Just after independence, the princely states were consolidated into the Indian union. Many royals entered politics and fought election on the basis of their wealth and royal background. Examples are: V.P. Singh (Raja of Manda, UP), Dinesh Singh (Raja of Kalakanter, UP), Rajkumakri Ratna Singh (Rajkumari of Kalakanter, UP, 1996 LS, 1999 LS), Abhai Pratap Singh (Bade Raja of Pratapgarh, UP), Sanjay Singh and Begum Noor Bana (Rampur Nawab family, UP, 1999 LS).

Poll Boycott

Deciding not to cast votes in election by a village, a community or a group is common in Indian electoral politics. Large-scale poll boycott is mostly observed in extremist, separatist and Naxalite affected areas. This type of situation helps a particular candidate or party to win election. For example, BJP gained in Ranchi and nearby areas due to poll boycott enforced by the Maoist Communist Centre (MCC) and People's War (PW) in 1990s. In these areas, poor tribals who are traditional supporters of Congress or the Left parties could not vote due to the boycott.

MP Fund Utilisation and Winning Elections: What Statistics Reveal

After identifying the enormous types of determinants of the election results of Lok Sabha general election and analysing the complexity of elections in India, it may not be prudent to waste precious time to find out the influence of these determinants empirically. However, let us not take any chance. In this section our objective is to test the commonly- held belief that the MP Fund helps the sitting MPs by providing an incumbency advantage over their contestants. This means, as they have a large sum of money at their disposal, they are in an advantageous position to meet the voters needs in terms of small developmental projects. As the sitting MPs are capable of funding hundreds of projects with the taxpayers' money, which his competitors do not have, the former have a better chance to win. To find out the truth empirically, we have followed a simple statistical method. Among all the MPs of the 12th and 13th Lok Sabha, we compare the utilisation of MPLADS funds by those MPs who won the election with that of those MPs who have lost.

It is expected that the funds utilisation would be better in case of the wining MPs in comparison to the losing MPs. Funds utilisation is measured in terms of two indicators - expenditure as a percentage of the sanctioned amount and expenditure as a percentage of the released amount. These figures are published by the Ministry of Statistics and Programme Implementation every month (http://mplads.nic.in/).

State-wise Comparison

Performance of MPs of 12th and 13th Lok Sabha in terms of MPLADS funds is depicted in Table 6.7. At all India level, 257 sitting MPs won the 1999 general election and 194 lost. Similarly, 218 sitting MPs won the 2004 general election and 191 lost. Contrary to the common belief, we found that the utilisation of funds by the MPs who have won the election is less than the MPs who have lost the elections in both the general elections. A state-wise analysis reveals that the findings are mixed. Out of 76 comparable-pairs of observations (state-wise won/lost, 1999 and 2004), 37 pairs confirm to the hypothesis and 39 pairs do not support the hypothesis. Thus we can conclude that, MP Fund utilisation does not provide any additional advantage to the sitting MPs for retaining the seat. A rigorous econometric analysis of the same data is made by using Logistic Regression Analysis and included in appendix. This analysis also arrived at the same conclusion.

Senior MPs and Junior MPs

Senior MPs are those who represent the LS in more than one occasion and because of their experience, leadership and popularity are elected from the same constituency repetitively. Because of this, they may not give the required importance to the MPLADS Fund utilisation. In Table 6.8 we have compared the performance of three-times continuously elected MPs of the

Table 6.7
MPLADS Utilisation and Election Winning: State-wise (1999 and 2004 General Election)

STATE/UT	*Status*	*1999 General Election*			*2004 General Election*		
		Number of Candidates	*Expenditure as % of Sanction*	*Expenditure as % of Release*	*Number of Candidates*	*Expenditure as % of Sanction*	*Expenditure as % of Release*
All India	NC	93	79.64	68.23	133	90.59	90.85
	Won	257	74.70	64.24	218	87.22	88.28
	Lost	194	77.00	66.43	191	88.46	89.93
	Total	544	76.34	65.69	542	88.28	88.81
Andhra Pradesh	NC	11	77.86	67.66	12	93.20	95.85
	Won	12	79.69	68.36	8	87.48	88.55
	Lost	19	68.88	60.76	22	85.95	88.53
	Total	42	74.28	64.75	42	88.35	90.67
Assam	NC	-	-	-	2	87.58	84.96
	Won	11	80.43	67.97	7	94.18	95.95
	Lost	3	80.80	60.37	5	92.58	93.03
	Total	14	80.50	66.36	14	92.68	93.31
Bihar	NC	7	84.56	77.08	10	87.32	84.74
	Won	23	82.1	70.69	10	90.27	90.16
	Lost	24	82.62	71.96	20	87.74	86.97
	Total	54	82.67	72.90	40	88.27	87.21
Gujarat	NC	-	-	-	3	90.71	86.77
	Won	14	61.92	55.21	14	90.48	89.03
	Lost	12	73.07	62.44	9	89.13	91.80
	Total	26	66.97	58.56	26	90.03	84.74
Haryana	NC	-	-	-	2	94.41	89.53
	Won	5	86.90	78.02	1	94.08	98.50
	Lost	5	83.32	69.59	7	99.31	97.85
	Total	10	85.22	73.90	10	97.82	96.23
Himachal Pradesh	NC	1	39.32	32.96	-	-	-
	Won	3	79.00	60.55	2	110.15	109.56
	Lost	-	-	-	2	109.34	103.98
	Total	4	68.40	53.65	4	109.74	106.63
Jammu & Kashmir	NC	1	0.00	0.00	2	69.30	67.99
	Won	3	62.42	46.56	2	79.71	76..92
	Lost	2	89.26	24.46	2	69.75	73.07
	Total	6	65.52	35.78	6	85.04	72.53
Karnataka	NC	2	83.03	66.55	8	95.52	98.22
	Won	13	69.86	55.26	12	100.65	100.65
	Lost	13	75.93	60.52	8	96.42	100.36
	Total	28	73.68	58.54	28	94.47	99.86
Kerala	NC	6	69.54	61.73	7	77.34	82.80
	Won	11	70.49	61.03	8	79.02	79.60
	Lost	3	77.73	67.58	4	84.29	85.68
	Total	20	71.28	62.21	19	79.51	82.07
Madhya Pradesh	NC	10	80.78	71.14	7	97.20	99.65
	Won	22	79.13	71.13	18	89.76	90.48
	Lost	8	76.76	71.11	4	91.94	93.92
	Total	40	79.04	71.13	29	91.89	93.17
Maharashtra	NC	10	73.27	64.22	8	89.33	89.48
	Won	19	64.12	56.17	24	81.27	84.89
	Lost	19	67.17	59.46	16	85.92	89.12
	Total	48	67.22	59.14	48	84.15	87.08
Orissa	NC	3	60.86	52.17	7	88.38	89.70
	Won	14	69.16	57.39	11	79.28	77.16
	Lost	4	83.52	67.15	3	82.39	78.78
	Total	21	70.65	58.55	21	82.79	81.50
Punjab	NC	2	76.64	57.16	5	86.34	86.44
	Won	3	78.14	64.07	4	82.61	84.25

Contd ...

Table 6.7 Contd ...

	Lost	8	81.71	62.64	4	74.45	76.43
	Total	13	80.04	62.11	13	81.33	82.55
Rajasthan	NC	5	80.44	64.80	5	96.32	97.47
	Won	8	68.77	52.41	13	94.85	99.71
	Lost	12	69.07	60.81	7	93.27	99.50
	Total	25	71.11	58.93	25	94.67	99.21
Tamil Nadu	NC	12	83.37	71.29	21	97.66	98.35
	Won	15	78.46	69.51	12	95.01	96.41
	Lost	12	80.88	76.28	6	98.77	101.01
	Total	39	80.67	72.21	39	97.00	98.15
Uttar Pradesh	NC	11	84.99	74.43	19	89.94	87.47
	Won	33	84.70	74.88	25	90.72	90.15
	Lost	41	82.42	71.34	36	89.94	87.47
	Total	85	84.05	73.13	80	90.15	88.34
West Bengal	NC	4	85.56	65.61	6	79.37	77.70
	Won	34	68.27	57.32	27	73.20	73.11
	Lost	4	59.05	48.53	9	75.94	77.95
	Total	42	68.81	57.23	42	72.07	72.20
Jharkhand	NC				-	-	-
	Won				1	81.32	82.57
	Lost				13	81.90	78.68
	Total				14	81.87	78.86
Chhatishgarh	NC				3	94.97	91.58
	Won				6	93.30	92.95
	Lost				2	102.22	103.69
	Total				11	95.38	94.57
Uttaranchal	NC				1	90.29	92.93
	Won				3	98.82	94.84
	Lost				1	91.34	97.00
	Total				5	95.34	94.89
Other States/Uts	NC	7	79.94	70.26	5	88.21	89.57
	Won	14	72.92	65.27	10	90.52	91.04
	Lost	5	78.45	65.02	11	91.84	90.44
	Total	26	75.69	66.43	26	90.60	90.51

Note: NC stands for 'not contested'. Expenditure, released and sanctioned amounts are calculated from the cumulative figures while considering the results of 1999 General Election. But, for considering the results of 2004 General Election, we have considered the net amounts (13th Lok Sabha time).

13th Lok Sabha (11th, 12th and 13th LS) with that of other MPs. It is observed that in case of both the senior MPs as well as junior MPs, the fund utilisation by the winning MPs is always less than those MPs who have lost the election. This again goes contrary to the popular belief that a MP looses the election because of non-utilisation of the MP Funds.

Major Political Parties

Indian National Congress (INC) and Bharatia Janata Party (BJP) are two major political parties who captured largest

Table 6.8
MPLADS Utilisation and Election Winning Senior MPs vs. Junior MPs of the 13th Lok Sabha (2004 General Election: All India)

	Three times continuous MPs			*Other MPs*		
	Number of candidates	*Expenditure as % of sanction*	*Expenditure as % of release*	*Number of candidates*	*Expenditure as % of sanction*	*Expenditure as % of release*
NC	14 (10.85%)	83.52	84.63	119 (28.81%)	91.41	91.57
Won	78 (60.46%)	85.94	85.94	140 (33.90%)	87.13	88.77
Lost	37 (28.68%)	88.71	89.50	154 (37.29%)	88.40	88.80
Total	129 (100.00%)	86.48	86.83	413 (100.00%)	88.82	89.58

Table 6.9
MPLADS Utilisation and Election Winning Major Political Parties of the 13th Lok Sabha (2004 General Election: All India)

STATE/UT	*Status*	*Number of candidates*	*Expenditure as % to sanction*	*Expenditure as % to release*
INC	NC	26	90.89	91.67
	Won	38	87.47	90.05
	Lost	46	91.75	93.56
	Total	110	90.07	91.92
BJP	NC	30	91.87	91.75
	Won	76	90.08	91.13
	Lost	76	87.99	87.96
	Total	182	89.49	89.89
Others	NC	78	90.03	90.27
	Won	106	84.00	84.54
	Lost	71	86.74	87.04
	Total	255	86.64	87.03

numbers of Lok Sabha seats in the 2004 general election. In order to get more insight into the influential factors that helped these parties to win election and the role played by the MP Fund in this process, we compared the MPLADS Fund utilisation between those MPs who won the election and those MPs who lost the election. Table 6.9 reveals that the fund utilisation status of the loosing MPs is relatively better in case of INC and other political parties in comparison to the winning MPs. Only in case of the BJP, the utilisation is poor in case of the MPs who have lost in comparison to MPs who have won. Thus the empirical results do not support the hypothesis that if the sitting MP spends better, the chance of winning the election is more.

Shift in Constituencies

An examination of the results of the 1999 general election and the 2004 general election also reveals that except a few parliamentary constituencies, in all others, change of political parties as well as individual is very common. Shift of constituencies from one party to other is depicted in the Figure 6.1.

Figure 6.1: Shift in Constituency

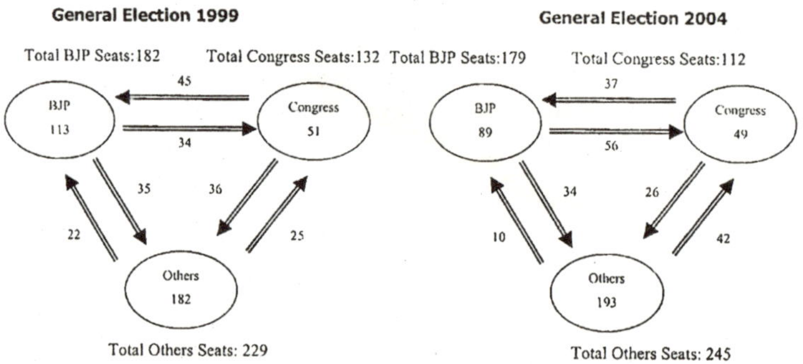

The INC could retain only 51 constituencies in the 1999 election and 49 constitutions in the 2004 election. This comes to only 38.64 per cent and 43.75 per cent of its constituencies. The other main political party, BJP, performed no better. It retained 113 constituencies in the 1999 election and 89 constituencies in the 2004 election. Which is only 62 per cent and 50 per cent of its constituencies respectively, though they were the ruling party during both the times. We also observe shuffling of constituencies amongst parties in sizable numbers. For example, the BJP lost 56 constituencies to INC but captured 37 back during the 2004 election. The purpose of depicting these results is to bring home the fact that despite the so-called MP Fund advantage, large scale shuffling of constituencies was observed in both the 1999 and 2004 elections. Table 6.7 also reveals that 194 seating MPs lost the 1999 election and 191 seating MPs lost the 2004 election.

Do Election and MP Funds Influence Each Other?

The first section of this chapter identified a number of factors that influence the election result. All these factors in combination determine the final election outcome. In the second section we tried to co-relate the utilisation of MP funds with that of the election result to find out the influence of the latter on the former. The empirical findings do not support our hypothesis that better utilisation of MP Funds leads to favourable election result for the incumbent MPs. We also found that a large numbers of seating MPs could not retain voters in their constituencies despite the so-called advantage of having the MP Fund. Now the question is does the political approach to local community need assessment and action (as depicted in Chapter 5) fails to deliver the intended result in the absence of a clear link between the MP Fund utilisation and election result?

The Fear of Loosing an Election

In democratic India, the executive power of governance is exercised by that political party or coalition of parties, which secures majority in the Lok Sabha. This is possible only when the party(s) capture majority of the constituencies by wining in the election. Even becoming an MP, though not of the ruling party, means a lot to a politician. Thus contesting and winning an election is the prime mover for a political leader. And he does not take any chance in so for as mobilisation of each and every effort is concerned. Where every vote counts and the stakes are high, no sitting MP would like to send a message that the MP Fund that they have, is either un-utilized or misutilized. Thus it is the fear of loosing the election that motivates the MPs to utilize the MP Fund judiciously. Aanalysis of Tables 6.7, 6.8 and 6.9 reveals that better utilisation of the MP Fund is not strongly associated with the election result. But it is also found that the differences observed in utilisation between the winning and the loosing candidates (MPs) are not much. Lastly, it is observed that the level of utilisation for both the winning and loosing candidates is as high as 90 percent. All these prompted us to believe the existence of reverse causality between MP Fund utilisation and election result. That is, the fear of loosing an election leads to better utilisation of the MP Funds, qualitatively as well as quantitatively, not the other way round.

7
MP Fund Scheme and People's Representatives

The whole exercise in the previous chapters hovers around a single theme- the direct role played by the Members of Parliament in community and local area development. The functions assigned to these MPs by the Constitution are described below.

The main function of both the Houses is to pass laws. Every Bill has to be passed by both the Houses and assented to by the President before it becomes law. The subjects over which Parliament can legislate are the subjects mentioned under the Union List in the Seventh Schedule to the Constitution of India. Broadly speaking, Union subjects are those important subjects which for reasons of convenience, efficiency and security are administered on all-India basis. The principal Union subjects are Defense, Foreign Affairs, Railways, Transport and Communications, Currency and Coinage, Banking, Customs and Excise Duties. There are numerous other subjects on which both Parliament and State Legislatures can legislate. Under this category mention may be made of economic and social planning, social security and insurance, labour welfare, price control and vital statistics. Besides passing laws, Parliament can by means of resolutions, motions for adjournment, discussions and questions addressed by members to Ministers exercise control over the administration of the country and safeguard people's liberties.

(source: www.parliamentofindia.nic.in / ls / intro / p1.htm)

Ever since the first elected Parliament came into being in April 1952, members of both the houses have been trying to influence the local administration. They have also been members of almost all committees, both statutory and otherwise, in their constituencies and exercise control over the administration to execute developmental and welfare projects. But the effectiveness of this arrangement is dependent on many factors: individual leadership quality, knowledge on government functioning, information of projects and programmes, equation with officials, political party in power in the state and district. Often the conflict between the top officials of the programme implementing agencies and the people's representatives are found to be common. So the latter were in search of maneuvering space for quite long. First the members of legislative assemblies got the chance in a few states and then in 1993 the MPs got the opportunity to execute a scheme called MPLADS, under which, each MP can execute projects worth Rs. 2 crore in their constituency every year. The rationale for such a scheme is that the MPs are in a better position to assess the local needs, prioritise them to allot the limited resources and execute them to harvest maximum benefits. In Chapter 5, we demonstrated in detail the political approach to local community need assessment and action and found that the MP Fund scheme is to a large extent follow this approach. Suggestions like making the funds lapsable and bringing in transparency in scheme implementation are made to make it effective.

The model of "political approach to local community need assessment and action" assumes that the political executives are people's representatives as they are directly elected by the eligible adult voters. But where should we place the Rajya Sabha members. Unlike LS members, the RS members are indirectly elected by the MLAs in accordance with the system of proportional representation by means of single transferable vote. Secondly, unlike the LS members who represent a parliamentary constituency, they represent the state. They are no doubt Members of Parliament, but not the people's representatives in the right sense. And this is probably why their performance in terms of MP Fund utilisation lags behind the LS MPs. There is little pressure on them to utilize the financial resources at their disposal. In preceding chapters we have also demonstrated how the works chosen by the RS MPs are quite different from the LS MPs. A comparison between the MPLAD works funded through the LS MPs and the RS MPs would lead us to the conclusion that the MP Fund scheme is basically designed for local community and area development through the LS MPs alone.

There are many more people's representatives along with the MPs. In India we have a three tier system of Panchayati Raj Institutions (PRIs) at the village, block and district level. We find in most of the states, directly elected peoples' representatives are the members of these PRIs. Thus the MPs along with the MLAs and the PRI representatives are operating in same area for the development and welfare of the communities. How in a federal democratic setup, all these people's representatives compete with each other to fund local area and community development was demonstrated in Chapter 4. The model of "political approach to local community need" assessment and action is true for MLAs and PRI representatives as well. Thus in the present federal political system, this type of competitive environment is good for the public. The MP Fund scheme strengthens the democratic federal system rather than weaken it. Like the invisible hands of the market, the competitive federalism at the local level would synchronise the developmental and welfare activities of all the people's representatives.

The MPs (mainly of LS), MLAs and the members of PRIs are peoples' representatives as they are elected by the people directly. The centrality of election within the framework of the "political approach to local community need assessment and action" was the main theme in this book. In Chapter 6 we found that even though the MP Fund scheme is one among hundreds of factors that determines election results, the MPs do not dare to neglect it. As the stake in political power is high for all types of people's representatives, it is expected that the use of tax payers' money would be made judiciously by them. They may or may not be benefited through the incumbency advantage, but, the fear of loosing the constituency is enough to bring all of them in conformity to the "political approach to local community need assessment and action".

APPENDIX
MP Fund Utilisation and Winning Election: an Econometric Analysis

While a statistical analysis was done to find out the influence of the MP Fund on the Lok Sabha election outcome, we used simple statistics like the expenditure as a percentage of sanctioned amounts and expenditure as a percentage of released amount. A comparison was made between the MPs those who won the election with the MPs those who lost the election. This was done state-wise and at the national level for both the 1999 and 2004 general elections. The results of such an analysis leads to the conclusion that "MP funds utilization does not provide any additional advantage to the sitting MPs for retaining the seat". However, one can apply rigorous econometrics method to find out the causal relationship between the MP fund utilization and election results. Here we use the Logistic Regression technique and fully rely on Scott Menard's monograph titled "Applied Logistic Regression Analysis", Sage Publications, 1995.

In this case, we have a dichotomous dependent variable called Lok Sabha Election Results (LSER). It takes two values; either 'win' or 'lost'. The two predictors are, (i) the expenditure as percentage to release (ExPcRel) and (ii) the expenditure as percentage to sanction (ExPcSanc). The functional relationship is expressed as followes:

$$\text{Logit } Y = \alpha + \beta_1 X_1 + \beta_2 X_2 \qquad \ldots (1)$$

$$\text{Logit (LSER)} = \alpha + \beta_1 \text{ (ExPcRel)} + \beta_2 \text{ (ExPcSanc)} \quad \text{... (2)}$$

LSER takes two values; 1 or 0

ExPcRel Maximum value: 128.09%

Minimum value: 42.88%

Average value: 88.28%

ExPcSanc Maximum value: 120.50%

Minimum value: 41.01%

Average value: 87.21%

Logistic Regression Out-put for Determinants of Election Result of 2004 Lok Sabha Election

Case Processing Summary

Unweighted Cases(a)		*N*	*Percent*
Selected Cases	Included in Analysis	410	100.0
	Missing Cases	0	.0
	Total	410	100.0
Unselected Cases		0	.0
Total		410	100.0

(a) If weight is in effect, see classification table for the total number of cases.

Dependent Variable Encoding

Original Value	*Internal Value*
0	0
1	1

Block 0: Beginning Block

Iteration History(a,b,c)

Iteration		*-2 Log likelihood*	*Coefficients*
			Constant
Step 0	1	566.731	0.127
	2	566.731	0.127

(a) Constant is included in the model.

(b) Initial -2 Log Likelihood: 566.731

(c) Estimation terminated at iteration number 2 because parameter estimates changed by less than 0.001.

Classification Table(a,b)

Observed			*Predicted*		
			Binary Dependent Variable Y		*Percentage Correct*
			0	1	
Step 0	Binary Dependent Variable Y	0	0	192	0.0
		1	0	218	100.0
	Overall Percentage				53.2

(a) Constant is included in the model.

(b) The cut value is 0.500

Variables in the Equation

		B	*S.E.*	*Wald*	*df*	*Sig.*	*Exp(B)*
Step 0	Constant	0.127	0.099	1.647	1	0.199	1.135

Variables not in the Equation

			Score	*df*	*Sig.*
Step 0	Variables	IndenpendentVariableX1	0.415	1	0.520
		IndenpendentVariableX2	1.120	1	0.290
	Overall Statistics		1.760	2	0.415

Block 1: Method = Enter

Iteration History (a, b, c, d)

Iteration		*-2 Log likelihood*	*Coefficients*		
			Constant	*Indenpendent VariableX1*	*Indenpendent VariableX2*
Step 1	1	564.966	0.739	0.013	-0.020
	2	564.966	0.746	0.013	-0.020
	3	564.966	0.746	0.013	-0.020

(a) Method: Enter

(b) Constant is included in the model.

(c) Initial -2 Log Likelihood: 566.731

(d) Estimation terminated at iteration number 3 because parameter estimates changed by less than 0.001.

Interpretation

The larger value of -2Log Likelihood indicates worse prediction of the dependent variable (LSER, won=1 and lost=0)

Omnibus Tests of Model Coefficients

		Chi-square	*df*	*Sig.*
Step 1	Step	1.765	2	0.414
	Block	1.765	2	0.414
	Model	1.765	2	0.414

Interpretation of Goodness of fit

If Gm or Chi-square is statically significant (ρ = 0.05), then we reject the null hypothesis, that $\beta_1=\beta_2=\beta_3=......\beta_k=0$, and conclude that information about the independent variable (ExPcRel and ExPcSanc) allows us to make better predictions of P(Y=h), (where h is some specific value, usually 1=won, and usually for a dichotomous dependent variable) than we could make without the independent variable. *The goodness of fit is found to be not statistically significant.*

Model Summary

Step	*-2 Log likelihood*	*Cox & Snell R Square*	*Nagelkerke R Square*
1	564.966(a)	0.004	0.006

A Estimation terminated at iteration number 3 because parameter estimates changed by less than 0.001.

Hosmer and Lemeshow Test

Step	*Chi-square*	*df*	*Sig.*
1	8.683	3	0.370

Contingency Table for Hosmer and Lemeshow Test

		Binary Dependent Variable Y = 0		Binary Dependent Variable Y = 1		
		Observed	Expected	Observed	Expected	Total
Step 1	1	21	21.508	20	19.492	41
	2	18	20.500	23	20.500	41
	3	19	20.093	22	20.907	41
	4	17	19.746	24	21.254	41
	5	23	19.429	18	21.571	41
	6	25	19.068	16	21.932	41
	7	20	18.735	21	22.265	41
	8	15	18.325	26	22.675	41
	9	20	17.820	21	23.180	41
	10	14	16.776	27	24.224	41

Classification Table(a)

			Predicted		
			Binary Dependent Variable Y		Percentage Correct
Observed			0	1	
Step 1	Binary Dependent Variable Y	0	29	163	15.1
		1	29	189	86.7
	Overall Percentage				53.2

(a) The cut value is 0.500.

Interpretation of Classification/Contingent table

The contingent tables indicate the predictive efficiency of the model. When all cases are correctively predicted, $\phi\rho = 1$, otherwise, $\phi\rho < 1$, even when the maximum possible number of cases for a given set of marginals is correctly classified.

$$\phi\rho = (ab - bc)/ \tfrac{1}{2}((a + b)(b + d) + (c + d)(a + c))$$

Where, a= 189, b= 29, c= 163 and d= 29

The low value of $\phi\rho = 0.0005$ indicates that the cases are not correctly predicted.

Variables in the Equation

(a) Variable(s) entered on step 1: IndenpendentVariable X1, Indenpendent Variable X2.

		B	S.E.	Wald	df	Sig.	Exp(B)	95.0% C.I.for EXP(B)	
								Lower	Upper
Step 1(a)	Independent VariableX1	.013	.016	.638	1	.425	1.013	.981	1.046
	Independent VariableX2	-.020	.017	1.342	1	.247	.980	.947	1.014
	Constant	.746	.634	1.386	1	.239	2.109		

Interpretation of the variables in the Equation

Logit (LSER = 1) = 0.746 + 0.013 (ExPcRel) + 0.02 (ExPcSanc) ... (3)

Odds (LSER = 1) = $e^{\alpha + \beta 1 \text{ (ExPcRel)} + \beta 2 \text{ (ExPcSanc)}}$ ... (4)

where e is natural log

Odds (LSER = 1) = $e^{0.746 + 0.013 \text{ (ExPcRel)} + 0.02 \text{ (ExPcSanc)}}$ ... (5)

Probabilities of (LSER = 1) = $(e^{\alpha + \beta 1 \text{ (ExPcRel)} + \beta 2 \text{ (ExPcSanc)}}) / (1+ e^{\alpha + \beta 1 \text{ (ExPcRel)} + \beta 2 \text{ (ExPcSanc)}})$ ... (6)

Probabilities of (LSER = 1) = $(e^{0.746 + 0.013 \text{ (ExPcRel)}+0.02\text{(ExPcSanc)}})/ (1+ e^{0.746 + 0.013 \text{ (ExPcRel)} + 0.02 \text{ (ExPcSanc)}})$ ... (7)

"It is important to understand that the probabilities, the odds, and the logit are three different ways of expressing exactly the same thing. Of the three measures, the probabilities or the odds is probably the most easily understood" (Menanrd,1995: 13). For the sitting MP who has utilized the MP Funds the most (128.09% of expenditure to release and 120.50% of expenditure to sanction), the probability of winning the Lok Sabha election is fifty per cent. For the sitting MP who utilized the MP funds the least (42.88% of expenditure to release and 41.01% of expenditure to sanction) the probability of winning the Lok Sabha election is about sixty is to forty. This is going against the hypothesis that higher utilization of the MP funds leads to positive result in the election. Even for the MPs who utilize the average amount (88.28% of expenditure to release and 87.22% of expenditure to sanction) the probability of winning the Lok Sabha election is fifty-four is to forty-six. *Thus the logistic regression results do not support the hypothesis of direct and positive relationship of LSER with the ExPcRel and ExPcSanc. Secondly, the Wald statistics that are used to measure the statistical significance of the Logistic Regression Coefficients (βs) are also found to be statistically insignificant.*

Correlation Matrix

		Constant	*Indenpendent VariableX1*	*Indenpendent VariableX2*
Step 1	*Constant*	1.000	-.077	-.330
	IndenpendentVariableX1	-.077	1.000	-.914
	IndenpendentVariableX2	-.330	-.914	1.000

Release, Sanction and Expenditure of MPLADS Funds of XIII Lok Sabha MPs (Rs. In lakh)

Name of MPs	Constituency	Election Result	Net Release	Net Sanction	Net Expenditure	%Exp. to Release	%Exp. to Sanction
1	2	3	4	5	6	7	8
Andhra Pradesh							
S.VENUGOPAL CHARY	ADILABAD	Lost	750	675.6	695.5	92.73	102.95
GANTI VIJAYA KUMARI	AMALAPURAM(SC)	Not Cont	1150	1166	1198	104.17	102.74
DKALAVA SRINIVASULU	ANANTAPUR	Lost	1100	1156	1126.4	102.40	97.44
GANTA SRINIVASA RAO	ANAKAPALLI	Not Cont	1200	1159.6	1217.3	101.44	104.98
D. RAMA NAIDU	BAPATLA	Lost	1200	1293.4	1228.5	102.38	94.98
DUMPA MARY VIJAYA KUMARI	BHADRACHALAM(ST)	Not Cont	1200	1173.9	875.5	72.96	74.58
BOTCHA SATYANARAYANA	BOBBILI	Lost	1150	1172.6	1016.9	88.43	86.72
NOOTHANA KALVA RAMAKRISHNA REDDY	CHITTOOR	Not Cont	1100	1131.8	966.1	87.83	85.36
VIVEKANANDA REDDY Y.S.	CUDDAPAH	Won	1100	1059.2	1033.2	93.93	97.55
BOLLA BULLI RAMAIAH	ELURU	Lost	1150	1254.7	1049.2	91.23	83.62
YEMPARALA VENKATESWAR RAO	GUNTUR	Lost	1200	1210.6	869	72.42	71.78
CHADA SURESH REDDY	HANAMKONDA	Lost	1200	1276.8	924.6	77.05	72.42
B.K. PARTHASARATHI	HINDUPUR	Lost	1100	1206.2	1176.8	106.98	97.56
SULTAN SALAHUDDIN OWAISI	HYDERABAD	Won	800	746.9	651	81.38	87.16
MUDRAGADA PADMANABHAM	KAKINADA	Lost	1100	1153.7	1207	109.73	104.62
CHENNAMANENI VIDYASAGAR RAO	KARIMNAGAR	Lost	1200	1319.5	1055	87.92	79.95

RENUKA CHOWDHURY	KHAMMAM	Won	950	908.5	750.8	79.03	82.64
KAMBHALAPATI E. KRISHNA MURTHY	KURNOOL	Not Cont	1150	1209.4	1117.1	97.14	92.37
AMBATI BRAHMANAIAH	MACHILIPATNAM	Lost	1200	1223	935.9	77.99	76.52
A.P. JITHENDER REDDY	MAHABUBNAGAR	Not Cont	1200	1113.1	1164.1	97.01	104.58
A. NARENDRA	MEDAK	Won	1200	1296.6	1146.5	95.54	88.42
JAIPAL REDDY SUDINI	MIRYALGUDA	Won	1150	1241.6	925.8	80.50	74.57
MANDA JAGANNATH	NAGARKURNOOL(SC)	Won	1150	1093.5	1109.6	96.49	101.47
GUTHA SUKENDER REDDY	NALGONDA	Not Cont	1150	1236.9	1093.8	95.11	88.43
BHUMA NAGI REDDY	NANDYAL	Lost	1150	1167	1081.8	94.07	92.70
JANARDHANA REDDY NEDURUMALLI	NARASAPET	Won	1100	1092.4	774.7	70.43	70.92
UPPALAPATI VENKATA KRISHNAMRAJU	NARASAPUR	Lost	1300	1162.5	925	71.15	79.57
RAJESWARAMMA VUKKALA	NELLORE(SC)	Not Cont	1200	1264.9	970.6	80.88	76.73
GANGA REDDY GADDAM	NIZAMABAD	Not Cont	1200	1287.2	1308.3	109.03	101.64
KARANAM BALIRAMA KRISHNA MURTHY	ONGOLE	Not Cont	1150	1164.8	1236.1	107.49	106.12
DADICHILUKA VEERA GOURI SANKARA RAO	PARVATHIPURAM(ST)	Lost	1200	1308.1	747.7	62.31	57.16
SMT.C. SUGUNA KUMARI	PEDDAPALLI(SC)	Lost	1200	1200.2	827.7	68.98	68.96
SATYANARAYANA RAO S.B.P.B.K.	RAJAHMUNDRY	Lost	1150	1161	1044	90.78	89.92
GUNIPATI RAMAIAH	RAJAMPET	Lost	1100	1097.4	1099.3	99.94	100.17
BANDARU DATTATRAYA	SECUNDERABAD	Lost	1150	1178.4	1239.6	107.79	105.19
M. RAJAIAH	SIDDIPET(SC)	Not Cont	1200	1276.3	1227.8	102.32	96.20
KINJARAPU YERRANNAIDU	SRIKAKULAM	Won	1150	1265.9	1223.6	106.40	96.66
UMMAREDDY VENKATESWARLU	TENALI	Lost	1200	1240.5	1051	87.58	84.72

N. VENKATASWAMY	TIRUPATHI(SC)	Lost	1150	1235.1	945.9	82.25	76.58
GADDE RAMA MOHAN	VIJAYAWADA	Not Cont	1100	1214	1044.9	94.99	86.07
M.V.V.S. MURTHY	VISAKHAPATNAM	Lost	1150	1108.9	1241.5	107.96	111.96
BODAKUNTI VENKATESHWARLU	WARANGAL	Lost	1050	1100.2	774.6	73.77	70.41
Arunachal Pradesh							
WANGCHA RAJKUMAR	ARUNACHAL EAST	Lost	1200	1273.2	1436.4	119.70	112.82
JARBOM GAMLIN	ARUNACHAL WEST	Not Cont	1200	1167.3	974.5	81.21	83.48
Assam							
JAYANTA RONGPI	AUTO. DISTRICT(ST)	Lost	1100	1215.4	1262.7	114.79	103.89
A.F. GOLAM OSMANI	BARPETA	Won	1150	1175.4	914.4	79.51	77.79
ABDUL HAMID	DHUBRI	Not Cont	1200	1183	1023	85.25	86.48
PABAN SINGH GHATOWAR	DIBRUGARH	Lost	1200	1120.7	1091.5	90.96	97.39
BIJOYA CHAKRAVARTY	GUWAHATI	Not Cont	1150	1096.5	973.6	84.66	88.79
BIJOY KRISHNA HANDIQUE	JORHAT	Won	1200	1082.2	1194.7	99.56	110.40
DIP GOGOI	KALIABOR	Won	1050	1212.1	1135.3	108.12	93.66
NEPAL CHANDRA DAS	KARIMGANJ (SC)	Lost	1100	1111.7	809.4	73.58	72.81
SANSUMA KHUNGGUR BWISMUTHIARY	KOKRAJHAR (ST)	Won	1250	1173	1155.1	92.41	98.47
RANEE NARAH	LAKHIMPUR	Lost	1200	1172	1034.6	86.22	88.28
MADHAB RAJBANGSHI	MANGALDOI	Lost	1250	1259.1	1244.5	99.56	98.84
RAJEN GOHAIN	NOWGONG	Won	1150	1248.6	953.8	82.94	76.39
SONTOSH MOHAN DEV	SILCHAR	Won	1150	1222.5	1278.3	111.16	104.56

MONI KUMAR SUBBA	TEZPUR	Won	1100	1087.5	1092.9	99.35	100.50
Bihar							
SUKDEO PASWAN	ARARIA(SC)	Won	1150	1132.7	1085.7	94.41	95.85
RAM PRASAD SINGH	ARRAH	Not Cont	1050	1002	949.7	90.45	94.78
SHYAMA SINGH	AURANGABAD	Not Cont	1150	1115.4	763.4	66.38	68.44
MAHENDRA BAITHA	BAGAHA(SC)	Lost	1200	1264	1025.7	85.48	81.15
RAMJIVAN SINGH	BALIA	Lost	1100	1121.1	1159.2	105.38	103.40
DIGVIJAY SINGH	BANKA	Lost	850	758.6	898.2	105.67	118.40
NITISH KUMAR	BARH	Won	950	985.1	900.8	94.82	91.44
RAJO SINGH	BEGUSARAI	Not Cont	1100	1038.1	1144	104.00	110.20
MADAN PRASAD JAISWAL	BETTIAH	Not Cont	1200	1258.7	1084.3	90.36	86.14
SUBODH RAY	BHAGALPUR	Lost	1150	1107.6	1148.7	99.89	103.71
KANTI SINGH	BIKRAMGANJ	Not Cont	900	842.6	549.4	61.04	65.20
LALMUNI CHAUBEY	BUXAR	Won	1050	1102.9	911.1	86.77	82.61
RAJIV PRATAP RUDI	CHAPRA	Lost	1250	1238.4	905.7	72.46	73.13
KIRTI AZAD	DARBHANGA	Lost	1150	1178.2	1038.9	90.34	88.18
RAMJI MANJHI	GAYA (SC)	Not Cont	1000	919	785	78.50	85.42
RAGHUNATH JHA	GOPALGANJ	Not Cont	1000	951.9	913.2	91.32	95.93
RAM VILAS PASWAN	HAJIPUR(SC)	Won	1200	1064.7	1085.7	90.48	101.97
ARUN KUMAR	JAHANABAD	Lost	1050	965.9	864	82.29	89.45
DEVENDRA PRASAD YADAV	JHANJHARPUR	Won	1200	1265.7	1147.9	95.66	90.69
NIKHIL KUMAR CHOUDHARY	KATIHAR	Won	1200	1248.1	1005.8	83.82	80.59

RENU KUMARI	KHAGARIA	Lost	1200	1193.3	1111.7	92.64	93.16
SYED SHAHNAWAZ HUSSAIN	KISHANGANJ	Lost	1150	1132.7	991.2	86.19	87.51
SHARAD YADAV	MADHEPURA	Lost	1150	1079.7	835.7	72.67	77.40
HUKUMDEO NARAYAN YADAV	MADHUBANI	Lost	1100	1213.8	1149.3	104.48	94.69
PRABHUNATH SINGH	MAHARAJGANJ	Won	1200	1307.3	1116.4	93.03	85.40
Bramhanand Mandal	MONGHYR	Lost	1200	1107.5	1002.5	83.54	90.52
RADHA MOHAN SINGH	MOTIHARI	Lost	1200	1244.5	1119.3	93.28	89.94
CAPTAIN JAINA.PD. NISHAD	MUZAFFARPUR	Not Cont	1150	1139.2	1101	95.74	96.65
GEORGE FERNANDES	NALANDA	Not Cont	1250	1295.5	1140.6	91.25	88.04
SANJAY PASWAN	NAWADA(SC)	Lost	1050	1030.5	843.9	80.37	81.89
C.P. THAKUR	PATNA	Lost	1000	1004.3	808.5	80.85	80.50
RAM CHANDRA PASWAN	ROSERA(SC)	Won	1050	959.2	768.8	73.22	80.15
DINESH CHANDRA YADAV	SAHARSA	Lost	1200	1197.8	934.9	77.91	78.05
MANJAY LAL	SAMASTIPUR	Not Cont	1200	1111.6	890.9	74.24	80.15
MUNI LALL	SASARAM(SC)	Lost	1050	1060.2	954.3	90.89	90.01
MD ANWARUL HAQUE	SHEOHAR	Lost	1150	1148.7	976.7	84.93	85.03
NAWAL KISHORE RAI	SITAMARHI	Lost	1050	1020.3	766.5	73.00	75.12
M. SAHABUDDIN	SIWAN	Won	1150	1103.3	1072.6	93.27	97.22
RAGHUVANSH PRASAD SINGH	VAISHALI	Won	850	817.6	823.8	96.92	100.76
RAJESH RANJAN	PURNEA	Lost	1150	1136.7	947.5	82.39	83.36
Goa							
ANGLE RAMAKANT SOIRU	MORMUGAO	Lost	1100	1165.6	955.6	86.87	81.98

SHRIPAD VASSO NAIK	PANAJI	Won	1100	1150.1	697.1	63.37	60.61
Gujarat							
HARIN PATHAK	AHMEDABAD	Won	1100	1044.4	1009.3	91.75	96.64
DILEEP SANGHANI	AMRELI	Lost	1100	1163.4	1007.4	91.58	86.59
PATEL DIPAKBHAI CHIMANBHAI (SATHI)	ANAND	Not Cont	1000	960.7	972.2	97.22	101.20
CHAUDHARI HARIBH AI PARATHIBHAI	BANASKANTHA	Lost	1050	1120.8	1021	97.24	91.10
JAYABEN THAKKAR	BARODA	Won	1150	1232.9	961.6	83.62	77.99
RAJU RANA	BHAVNAGAR	Won	950	959.7	830.8	87.45	86.57
MANSU-KHBHAI VASAVA	BROACH	Won	1200	1158.7	1125.1	93.76	97.10
MANIBHAI RAMJIBHAI CHAUDHARI	BULSAR(ST)	Lost	1050	1092.9	1200.4	114.32	109.84
RAMSINH RATHAWA	CHHOTA UDAIPUR(ST)	Lost	1100	1195.7	938.8	85.35	78.51
VARMA RATILAL KALIDAS	DHANDHUKA(SC)	Won	1150	1116.2	1038.3	90.29	93.02
KATARA BABUBHAI KHIMABHAI	DOHAD(ST)	Won	1200	1270	1173.5	97.79	92.40
LALKRISHNA ADVANI (L.K.ADVANI)	GANDHINAGAR	Won	1050	1010.3	991	94.38	98.09
SOLANKI BHUPEN- DRASINH PRABHATSINH	GODHRA	Won	1150	1128	1050.8	91.37	93.16
CHANDRESH PATEL	JAMNAGAR	Lost	1100	1182.3	1038.8	94.44	87.86
CHIKHALIAY BHAVNABEN DEVRAJBHA	JUNAGADH	Lost	1150	1105.4	971.5	84.48	87.89
DINSHA PATEL	KAIRA	Won	1150	1128	882	76.70	78.19
VAGHELA SHANKARSINH LAXMANSINH	KAPADVANJ	Won	1200	1210.5	1118.2	93.18	92.38
GADHVI PUSHPADAN SAMBHUDAN	KUTCH	Won	1050	923	830.5	79.10	89.98
PATEL MANSINHBHAI KALYANJI	MANDVI(ST)	Lost	900	880	747.4	83.04	84.93
PUNJAJI SADAJI THAKOR	MEHSANA	Not Cont	850	859.4	680.4	80.05	79.17

RASHTRAPAL PRAVINCHANDRA SOMABH	PATAN(SC)	Lost	1050	1104.4	1033.5	98.43	93.58
JAVIYA GORDHAN- BHAI JADAVBHAI	PORBANDAR	Not Cont	1050	954	864	82.29	90.57
KATHIRIYA VALLABHBHAI RAMJIBHA	RAJKOT	Won	1150	1064.9	980.4	85.25	92.06
MADHUSUDAN DEVRAMMISTRY	SABARKANTHA	Won	1150	1194.1	1037.1	90.18	86.85
KASHIRAM RANA	SURAT	Won	1000	958.9	905.8	90.58	94.46
MAKWANA SAVSHIBHAI KANJIBHAI	SURENDRANAGAR	Lost	1100	1042	854.3	77.66	81.99
Haryana							
AJAY SINGH CHAUTALA	BHIWANI	Lost	1200	1169	1144	95.33	97.86
RAM CHANDER BAINDA	FARIDABAD	Lost	1150	1175.4	1103.9	95.99	93.92
SURENDER SINGH BARWALA	HISSAR	Lost	1100	1016.3	941.4	85.58	92.63
I D SWAMI	KARNAL	Lost	1000	984	1089.7	108.97	110.74
PROF KAILASHO DEVI	KURUKSHETRA	Not Cont	1200	1057	932.3	77.69	88.20
SUDHA YADAV	MAHENDRAGARH	Lost	1150	1122.8	1182.2	102.80	105.29
INDER SINGH	ROHTAK	Not Cont	1100	1124	1126.9	102.45	100.26
SUSHIL KUMAR INDORA	SIRSA(SC)	Lost	1200	1114.8	1167.9	97.33	104.76
KISHAN SINGH SANGWAN	SONEPAT	Won	1100	1151.6	1083.5	98.50	94.09
RATTAN LAL KATARIA	AMBALA (SC)	Lost	1200	1300.3	1199.3	99.94	92.23
Himachal Pradesh							
SURESH CHANDEL	HAMIRPUR	Won	1000	1003.7	1003.7	100.37	100.00
SHANTA KUMAR	KANGRA	Lost	950	854.4	1025.6	107.96	120.04
MAHESHWAR SINGH	MANDI	Lost	1250	1237.6	1262	100.96	101.97
COL. DHANI RAM SHANDIL	SHIMLA(SC)	Won	1000	985.5	1187.5	118.75	120.50

Jammu & Kashmir							
ALI MOHD NAIK	ANANTNAG	Not Cont	1250	1198.1	1009.4	80.75	84.25
ABDUL RASHID SHAHEEN	BARAMULLAH	Won	1000	1000	893	89.30	89.30
TALIB HUSSAIN	JAMMU	Not Cont	1100	1107.3	588.3	53.48	53.13
HASSAN KHAN	LADAKH	Lost	1300	1475.9	849	65.31	57.52
OMAR ABDULLAH	SRINAGAR	Won	1150	1074.6	760.7	66.15	70.79
CHAMAN LAL GUPTA	UDHAMPUR	Lost	1050	986	868.1	82.68	88.04
Karnataka							
R.S. PATIL	BAGALKOT	Lost	1200	1283.6	965.6	80.47	75.23
C.K. JAFFER SHARIEF	BANGALORE NORTH	Lost	1200	1217	1227.1	102.26	100.83
ANANTH KUMAR	BANGALORE SOUTH	Won	1150	1091.2	1194.1	103.83	109.43
AMARSINH VASANTARAO PATIL	BELGAUM	Lost	1050	1189.1	1306.5	124.43	109.87
KOLUR BASAVANAGOUD	BELLARY	Not Cont	1100	1148	988.2	89.84	86.08
RAMCHANDRA VEERAPPA	BIDAR (SC)	Won	1050	1269.2	1039.2	98.97	81.88
BASANGOUDA RAMAN- GOUDA PATIL	BIJAPUR	Won	1100	1246.4	1049.6	95.42	84.21
V. SREENIVASAPRASAD	CHAMARAJANAGAR(SC)	Not Cont	1150	1257.7	943.5	82.04	75.02
R.L. JALAPPA	CHIKBALLAPUR	Won	1100	1287	1409	128.09	109.48
JIGAJINAGI RAMESH CHANDAPPA	CHIKKODI(SC)	Won	1200	1338	1403.2	116.93	104.87
D.C. SRIKANTAPPA	CHIKMAGALUR	Won	1150	1210	1251.9	108.86	103.46
SHASHI KUMAR	CHITRADURGA	Not Cont	1200	1286.8	1326	110.50	103.05
G. MALLIKARJUNAPPA	DAVANGERE	Not Cont	1150	1224.5	1198.6	104.23	97.88
VIJAY SANKESHWAR	DHARWAD NORTH	Not Cont	1150	1212	1120.7	97.45	92.47

PROF. I.G. SANADI	DHARWAD SOUTH	Lost	1200	1174.4	1175.2	97.93	100.07
IQBAL AHEMED SARADGI	GULBARGA	Won	1150	1464.4	1184.9	103.03	80.91
G.PUTTA SWAMY GOWDA	HASSAN	Not Cont	1150	1033.1	922.4	80.21	89.28
H.D. DEVEGOWDA	KANAKAPURA	Won	1000	1038.7	1176.1	117.61	113.23
ALVA MARGARET	KANARA	Lost	1200	1300.6	1204.4	100.37	92.60
K.H. MUNIYAPPA	KOLAR(SC)	Won	1150	1169.1	493.1	42.88	42.18
H.G. RAMULU	KOPPAL	Not Cont	1150	1124.5	1339.9	116.51	119.16
AMBAREESH AMARANATHA.M.H	MANDYA	Won	1150	1303.7	1134.5	98.65	87.02
V. DHANANJAYA KUMAR	MANGALORE	Not Cont	1000	1019.4	1050	105.00	103.00
SRIKANTADATTA NARA - SIMHARAJA WADIYAR	MYSORE	Lost	1050	954.7	1033.9	98.47	108.30
A. VENKATESH NAIK	RAICHUR	Won	1150	1106.2	1142.1	99.31	103.25
S. BANGARAPPA	SHIMOGA	Won	700	680	658	94.00	96.76
G.S. BASAVARAJ	TUMKUR	Lost	1150	1297.5	1121.2	97.50	86.41
VINAY KUMAR SORAKE	UDUPI	Lost	1150	1159.6	1199.8	104.33	103.47
Kerala							
KODIKUNNIL SURESH	ADOOR(SC)	Lost	1200	1171	801.9	66.83	68.48
V.M. SUDHEERAN	ALAPPUZHA	Lost	1100	1178.7	1216.5	110.59	103.21
A. K. PREMAJAM	BADAGARA	Not Cont	1150	1211.5	746.5	64.91	61.62
K. MURALEEDHARAN	CALICUT(KOZHIKODE)	Not Cont	1150	1273.6	1098.7	95.54	86.27
A.P. ABDULLAKKUTTY	CANNANORE(KANNUR)	Won	1150	1177	969	84.26	82.33
VARKALA RADHAKRISHNAN	CHIRAYINKIL	Won	1250	1233.1	782.4	62.59	63.45
SEBASTIAN POUL	ERNAKULAM	Won	1200	1309.7	979.8	81.65	74.81

K. FRANCIS GEORGE	IDUKKI	Won	1100	1139	1050.7	95.52	92.25
T. GOVINDAN	KASARAGOD	Not Cont	1100	1121	1029.2	93.56	91.81
SURESH KURUP	KOTTAYAM	Not Cont	1150	1265.1	1085.2	94.37	85.78
E. AHAMED	MANJERI	Not Cont	1200	1301	944.2	78.68	72.57
RAMESH CHENNITHALA	MAVELIKARA	Lost	1150	1284	1116	97.04	86.92
K. KARUNAKARAN	MUKUNDAPURAM	Not Cont	1000	993.8	840.7	84.07	84.59
P.C. THOMAS	MUVATTUPUZHA	Won	1050	1135	1061	101.05	93.48
N. N. KRISHNADAS	PALAKKAD	Won	1050	980.9	816	77.71	83.19
BANATWALLA	PONNANI	Not Cont	1050	1184.5	713.6	67.96	60.24
P. RAJENDRAN	QUILON(KOLLAM)	Won	1150	1186	791.9	68.86	66.77
A. C. JOSE	THRISSOOR(TRICHUR)	Lost	1150	1161.7	932.4	81.08	80.26
V. S. SIVAKUMAR	THIRUVANANTHAPURAM	Lost	1200	1215.3	1033.4	86.12	85.03
S. AJAYA KUMAR	OTTAPPALAM(SC)	Won	1150	1007	793.3	68.98	78.78
Madhya Pradesh							
PRAHLADSINGH PATEL	BALAGHAT	Not Cont	1100	1120.9	921.7	83.79	82.23
VIJAY KUMAR KHANDEL- WAL (MUNNI BHAIYA)	BETUL	Won	1100	1101.4	1065.8	96.89	96.77
RAM LAKHAN SINGH	BHIND	Won	1200	1146.1	972.2	81.02	84.83
UMA BHARTI	BHOPAL	Not Cont	1150	1132.2	1069.8	93.03	94.49
KAMALNATH	CHHINDWARA	Won	1150	1295	1081	94.00	83.47
RAMKRISHNA KUSMARIA	DAMOH	Won	1100	1085.7	1008.2	91.65	92.86
GAJENDRA SINGH RAJUKHEDI	DHAR(ST)	Not Cont	1100	1106.6	1109.3	100.85	100.24
JYOTIRADITYA SCINDIA	GUNA	Won	1150	1186.6	1018.4	88.56	85.83

JAIBHAN SINGH PAVAIYA	GWALIOR	Lost	850	830.3	911.2	107.20	109.74
SUNDAR LAL PATWA	HOSHANGABAD	Not Cont	1050	1047	1084	103.24	103.53
SUMITRA MAHAJAN	INDORE	Won	1100	1142.5	1215.4	110.49	106.38
JAISHREE BANER- JEE (BHABHIJI)	JABALPUR	Not Cont	1100	1097.4	1260.9	114.63	114.90
KANTILAL BHURIYA	JHABUA(ST)	Won	1050	1021.6	938.2	89.35	91.84
SATYAVRAT CHAT - URVEDI(VINOD BHA YA)	KHAJURAHO	Lost	1050	1129.8	1081.5	103.00	95.72
NANDKUMAR SINGH CHOUHAN(NANDU BHAIYA	KHANDWA	Won	1150	1142.2	1031.4	89.69	90.30
TARACHAND PATEL	KHARGONE	Lost	1100	1144	873.3	79.39	76.34
FAGGAN SINGH KULASTE	MANDLA(ST)	Won	1100	1175	1047.4	95.22	89.14
LAKSHAMINARAYAN PANDEY	MANDSAUR	Won	1100	1043	990.7	90.06	94.99
ASHOK CHHAVIRAM ARGAL	MORENA(SC)	Won	1100	1156.5	1049.7	95.43	90.77
LAXMAN SINGH	RAJGARH	Won	1200	1280.6	1060.2	88.35	82.79
SUNDER LAL TIWARI	REWA	Lost	1150	1135.4	1031.8	89.72	90.88
VIRENDRA KUMAR	SAGAR(SC)	Won	1150	1038	1011.2	87.93	97.42
RAMANAND SINGH	SATNA	Not Cont	1200	1327.2	1374.3	114.53	103.55
RAM NARESH TRIPATHI	SEONI	Not Cont	1150	1216.4	1003	87.22	82.46
DALPAT SINGH	SHAHDOL (ST)	Won	1150	1141	994.5	86.48	87.16
THAVARCHAND GEHLOT	SHAJAPUR(SC)	Won	1100	1112.3	820.9	74.63	73.80
CHANDRA PRATAP SINGH (BABA SAHAB)	SIDHI(ST)	Won	1100	1174.9	1026.6	93.33	87.38
SATYANARAYAN JATIYA	UJJAIN(SC)	Won	900	881	898.1	99.79	101.94
SHIVRAJ SINGH	VIDISHA	Won	1100	1035.9	866.8	78.80	83.68

Maharastra							
DILIPKUMAR MANSUKHLAL GANDHI	AHMEDNAGAR	Not Cont	1150	1177	864	75.13	73.41
AMBEDKAR PRAKASH YASHWANT	AKOLA	Lost	1050	1039.3	702.3	66.89	67.57
GUDHE ANANT MAHADEOAPPA	AMRAVATI	Won	1150	1161.7	807.8	70.24	69.54
CHANDRAKANT KHAIRE	AURANGABAD	Won	1100	1179.1	1091.4	99.22	92.56
PAWAR SHARADCHAN DRA GOVINDRAO	BARAMATI	Won	1200	1317.8	1000.1	83.34	75.89
CHUNNILALBHAU THAKUR	BHANDARA	Not Cont	1150	1145.1	936.8	81.46	81.81
JAISINGRAO GAIKWAD PATIL	BEED	Won	1050	1057.1	975.3	92.89	92.26
RAM NAIK	MUMBAI NORTH	Lost	1000	1024.3	783.4	78.34	76.48
MONOHAR GAJANAN JOSHI	MUMBAI NORTH CENTRAL	Lost	1100	1144.5	1058	96.18	92.44
KIRIT SOMAIYA	MUMBAI NORTH EAST	Lost	1200	1300.3	1158.6	96.55	89.10
SUNIL DUTT	MUMBAI NORTH WEST	Won	1150	1211.6	1108.7	96.41	91.51
JAYAWANTI MEHTA	MUMBAI SOUTH	Lost	1050	1138.3	835.4	79.56	73.39
MOHAN VISHNU RAWALE	MUMBAI SOUTH CENTRAL	Won	1150	1337.6	1042.1	90.62	77.91
ADSUL ANANDRAO VITHOBA	BULDHANA(SC)	Won	1050	1108.8	816.6	77.77	73.65
PUGLIA NARESHKUM AR CHUNNALAL	CHANDRAPUR	Lost	1050	1049.5	1304.8	124.27	124.33
DIWATHE NAMDEO HARBAJI	CHIMUR	Not Cont	1150	1138.9	965.7	83.97	84.79
ADV CHINTAMAN WANAGA	DAHANU(ST)	Lost	1100	1079	943.1	85.74	87.41
RAMDAS RUPLA GAVIT	DHULE (ST)	Lost	1200	1235.4	1086.3	90.53	87.93
ANNASAHEB M.K. PATIL	ERANDOL	Won	1150	1224.8	876.8	76.24	71.59
MANE SHIVAJI GYANBARAO	HINGOLI	Lost	1150	1196.8	1014.7	88.23	84.78
MANE NIVEDITA SAMBHAJIRAO	ICHALKARANJI	Won	1150	1229.3	1221.6	106.23	99.37

Y.G. MAHAJAN (SIR)	JALGAON	Won	1150	1303.1	1025	89.13	78.66
DANVE RAOSAHEB DADARAO PATIL	JALNA	Won	1100	1155.5	816.1	74.19	70.63
SHRINIWAS DADAS- AHEB PATIL(MARULKAR)	KARAD	Won	1150	1286.8	1115.6	97.01	86.70
ASHOK NAMDEORAO MOHOL	KHED	Lost	1200	1307.1	1053.1	87.76	80.57
RAMSHETH THAKUR	KULABA	Not Cont	1150	1133.1	1226.8	106.68	108.27
MANDLIK SADASHIV RAO DADOBA	KOLHAPUR	Won	1100	1173.5	1102.9	100.26	93.98
E V ALIAS BALA- SAHEB VIKHE PATIL	KOPARGAON	Won	1050	1042.2	834	79.43	80.02
PATIL SHIVRAJ VISHWANATH	LATUR	Lost	1100	1278.4	1182.9	107.54	92.53
MAHALE HARIBHAU SHANKAR	MALEGAON(ST)	Lost	1150	1105.1	1116.3	97.07	101.01
VILAS MUTTEMWAR	NAGPUR	Won	800	783.4	391.2	48.90	49.94
KHATGAONKAR BHASKARRAO BAPURAO	NANDED	Lost	1100	1128	926.3	84.21	82.12
GAVIT MANIKRAO HODLYA	NANDURBAR(ST)	Won	1150	1102.3	783.7	68.15	71.10
DHIKALE UTTAMRAO NATHUJI	NASHIK	Not Cont	1150	1167.6	1113.6	96.83	95.38
KAMBLE SHIVAJI VITHALRAO	OSMANABAD(SC)	Not Cont	1100	1097	1003.9	91.26	91.51
ATHAWALE RAMDAS BANDU	PANDHARPUR(SC)	Won	1150	1147.5	1054.9	91.73	91.93
JADHAVE SURESH RAMRAO	PARBHANI	Not Cont	1150	1107.7	1065.7	92.67	96.21
PRADEEP RAWAT	PUNE	Lost	1200	1251.2	942	78.50	75.29
SURESH PRABHAKAR PRABHU	RAJAPUR	Won	1000	1045	884.2	88.42	84.61
SUBODH MOHITE	RAMTEK	Won	1200	1135.3	784.5	65.38	69.10
ANANT GANGARAM GEETE	RATNAGIRI	Won	1150	1279.9	1011.4	87.95	79.02
PRAKASH (BAPU) VASANTRAO PATIL	SANGLI	Won	1150	1110.6	1052.1	91.49	94.73
LAXMANRAO PAND- URANG JADHAV (PATIL)	SATARA	Won	1100	1132.8	1099.1	99.92	97.03

PRATAPSINH SHANKAR RAO	SOLAPUR	Not Cont	1150	1198.8	1011.2	87.93	84.35
PRAKASH PARANJPE	THANE	Won	1100	1202	958.5	87.14	79.74
PRABHA RAO	WARDHA	Lost	1150	1114.7	1009.8	87.81	90.59
BHAWANA PUNDLIKRAO GAWALI	WASHIM	Won	1250	1212.4	855.8	68.46	70.59
UTTAMRAO DEORAO PATIL	YAVATMAL	Lost	1200	1278.9	925.4	77.12	72.36
Manipur							
TH. CHAOBA	INNER MANIPUR	Lost	1100	1082.1	922.1	83.83	85.21
HOLKHOMANG HAOKIP	OUTER MANIPUR(ST)	Lost	1100	1056.1	812.3	73.85	76.92
Meghalaya							
PATY RIPPLE KYNDIAH	SHILLONG	Won	1000	966.2	966.2	96.62	100.00
PURNO AGITOK SANGMA	TURA	Won	1200	1126.8	1009.4	84.12	89.58
Mizoram							
VANLALZAWMA	MIZORAM (ST)	Won	1150	1192	1192	103.65	100.00
Nagaland							
K. ASUNGBA SANGTAM	NAGALAND	Lost	1000	805	850	85.00	105.59
Orissa							
KUMUDINI PATNAIK	ASKA	Not Cont	1050	1044.3	841.3	80.12	80.56
MAHAMEGHABAHAN AIRA KHARABELA SWAIN	BALASORE	Won	1150	1156.5	955.1	83.05	82.59
ANADICHARAN SAHU	BERHAMPUR	Lost	1100	1097	750.2	68.20	68.39
ARJUN CHARAN SETHI	BHADRAK(SC)	Won	1200	892.7	683.9	56.99	76.61
PROF. PRASANNA KUMAR PATASANI	BHUBANESWAR	Won	1250	1394.1	832.5	66.60	59.72
SANGEETA KUMARI SINGH DEO	BOLANGIR	Won	1100	1064	901.8	81.98	84.76

BHARTRUHARI MAHTAB	CUTTACK	Won	1150	1222.3	1245.5	108.30	101.90
DEBENDRA PRADHAN	DEOGARH	Not Cont	1150	1152.6	885.8	77.03	76.85
KAMAKHYA PRASAD SINGH DEO	DHENKANAL	Lost	1200	1123.3	951.3	79.28	84.69
TRILOCHAN KANUNGO	JAGATSINGHPUR	Not Cont	1150	1188.3	1128.2	98.10	94.94
JAGANNATH MALLIK	JAJPUR(SC)	Not Cont	1150	1170.7	1005.4	87.43	85.88
BIKRAM KESHARI DEO	KALAHANDI	Won	1200	1151.2	1050.1	87.51	91.22
PRABHAT KUMAR SAMANTRAY	KENDRAPARA	Not Cont	1000	1033	870.8	87.08	84.30
ANANTA NAYAK	KEONJHAR(ST)	Won	1150	1134	730.2	63.50	64.39
HEMA GAMMANG	KORAPUT(ST)	Not Cont	1200	1203	1294.2	107.85	107.58
SALKHAN MURMU	MAYURBHANJ (ST)	Lost	1150	1078.4	1016.5	88.39	94.26
PARSURAM MAJHI	NOWARANGPUR(ST)	Won	1200	1070.6	988.6	82.38	92.34
PADMANAVA BEHERA	PHULBANI(SC)	Not Cont	1050	1073.3	926.1	88.20	86.29
BRAJA KISHORE TRIPATHY	PURI	Won	950	890	639.3	67.29	71.83
PRASANNA ACHARYA	SAMBALPUR	Won	1000	1003.4	729.5	72.95	72.70
JUAL ORAM	SUNDARGARH (ST)	Won	1150	1187	889.6	77.36	74.95
Punjab							
RAGHUNANDAN LAL BHATIA	AMRITSAR	Won	800	889.7	699.4	87.43	78.61
BHAN SINGH BHAURA	BHATINDA (SC)	Not Cont	1200	1229.4	983	81.92	79.96
JAGMEET SINGH BRAR	FARIDKOT	Not Cont	800	870.7	560.2	70.03	64.34
ZORA SINGH	FIROZEPUR	Won	1200	1150.2	889.2	74.10	77.31
VINOD KHANNA	GURDASPUR	Won	850	884.5	884.5	104.06	100.00
CHARANJIT SINGH CHANNI	HOSHIARPUR	Not Cont	1100	1080.4	1102.3	100.21	102.03

BALBIR SINGH	JALANDHAR	Not Cont	1000	982.2	1105.8	110.58	112.58
GURCHARAN SINGH GALIB	LUDHIANA	Not Cont	1150	1093.8	787	68.43	71.95
PRENEET KAUR	PATIALA	Won	1100	1104	855	77.73	77.45
SANTOSH CHOWDHARY	PHILLAUR (SC)	Lost	1100	1116.6	1260.5	114.59	112.89
SHAMSHER SINGH	ROPAR (SC)	Lost	950	950.3	452.3	47.61	47.60
SIMRANJIT SINGH MANN	SANGRUR	Lost	1250	1339.9	1192.9	95.43	89.03
TIRLOCHAN SINGH TUR	TARAN TARAN	Lost	1150	1162	495.8	43.11	42.67
Rajasthan							
RASA SINGH RAWAT	AJMER	Won	1100	1077	1135.9	103.26	105.47
JASWANT SINGH YADAV	ALWAR	Not Cont	1150	1175.7	1205.4	104.82	102.53
TARA CHAND BHAGORA	BANSWARA(ST)	Not Cont	1100	1216.9	1198.7	108.97	98.50
COL SONARAM CHOWDHARY	BARMER	Lost	1200	1235.5	1298.9	108.24	105.13
BAHADUR SINGH KOLI	BAYANA(SC)	Not Cont	1150	1083.6	1096.6	95.36	101.20
VISHVENDRA SINGH	BHARATPUR	Won	1200	1156.3	1047.4	87.28	90.58
VIJYENDRA PAL SINGH	BHILWARA	Won	1100	1098.8	1071.8	97.44	97.54
RAMESHWAR LAL DUDI	BIKANER	Lost	1300	1437.7	1259	96.85	87.57
SHRICHAND KRIPLANI	CHITTORGARH	Won	1100	1081.9	1031	93.73	95.30
RAM SINGH KASWAN	CHURU	Won	1150	1218.1	1210	105.22	99.34
RAMA DEVI	DAUSA	Not Cont	1200	1171.1	967.4	80.62	82.61
NIHAL CHAND	GANGANAGAR(SC)	Won	1150	1271.6	1177	102.35	92.56
GIRDHARI LAL BHARGAVA	JAIPUR	Won	1150	1252.5	1037.6	90.23	82.84
BUTA SINGH	JALORE(SC)	Lost	1200	1268	1278.6	106.55	100.84

VASUNDHARA RAJE	JHALAWAR	Not Cont	1100	1121	1088.2	98.93	97.07
SISRAM OLA	JHUNJHUNU	Won	1150	1295.3	1157.9	100.69	89.39
JASWANT SINGH VISHNOI	JODHPUR	Won	1150	1142.1	1238.2	107.67	108.41
RAGHUVEER SINGH KOUSHAL	KOTA	Won	1200	1316.2	1211.5	100.96	92.05
RAM RAGHUNATH CHAUDHARY	NAGAUR	Lost	900	1071.8	800.8	88.98	74.72
PUSP JAIN	PALI	Won	1100	1371	1092	99.27	79.65
BHERU LAL MEENA	SALUMBAR(ST)	Lost	1200	1335.2	1299.8	108.32	97.35
JASKAUR MEENA	SAWAI MADHOPUR(ST)	Lost	1250	1185.4	1005.7	80.46	84.84
SUBHASH MAHARIA	SIKAR	Won	1150	1213	1248	108.52	102.89
KAILASH MEGHWAL	TONK(SC)	Won	1150	1117	1149.2	99.93	102.88
GIRIJA VYAS	UDAIPUR	Lost	1150	1214.2	1216.3	105.77	100.17
BHIM PD. DAHAL	SIKKIM	Not Cont	1150	1227.8	1179.8	102.59	96.09
Tamil Nadu							
JAGATHRAKSHAKAN S. DR.	ARAKKONAM	Not Cont	1200	1168.8	1141.9	95.16	97.70
MOORTHY A.K.	CHENGALPATTU	Won	1150	1214	1205	104.78	99.26
PONNUSWAMY E.	CHIDAMBARAM(SC)	Won	1100	1328.3	1257.8	114.35	94.69
RADHAKRISHNAN C.P.	COIMBATORE	Lost	1150	1134	972.3	84.55	85.74
SANKAR ADHI	CUDDALORE	Not Cont	1150	1190.5	1034.5	89.96	86.90
ELANGOVAN P.D.	DHARAMAURI	Lost	1050	1042.2	1103.3	105.08	105.86
SREENIVAASAN C.	DINDIGUL	Not Cont	1200	1118.8	1217	101.42	108.78
KALIAPPAN K.K.	GOBICHETTIPALAYAM	Not Cont	1100	1167	1225	111.36	104.97
CHINNASAMY M.	KARUR	Not Cont	1150	1084.6	1239	107.74	114.24

VETRISELVAN V.	KRISHNAGIRI	Not Cont	1200	1268	1254.9	104.58	98.97
MURASOLIMARAN	MADRAS CENTRAL	Not Cont	650	607.5	472.3	72.66	77.74
KUPPUSAMY C	MADRAS NORTH	Won	1250	1403.5	1313	105.04	93.55
BAALU T.R.	MADRAS SOUTH	Won	850	854.7	890	104.71	104.13
MOHAN P.	MADURAI	Won	1100	1134.1	1164	105.82	102.64
MANI SHANKAR AIYAR	MAYILADUTURAI	Won	1200	1181.1	1069.6	89.13	90.56
VIJAYAN A.K.S.	NAGAPATHINAM(SC)	Won	1050	930	854.4	81.37	91.87
RADHAKRISHNAN P.	NAGARCOIL	Lost	1000	941.9	995.5	99.55	105.69
MATHAN M. ALIAS MASTER MATHAN M.	NILGIRIS	Lost	1150	1231	1121.8	97.55	91.13
KUMARASAMY P.	PALANI	Not Cont	1150	1156.3	1088.2	94.63	94.11
DHINKARAN	PERIYAKULAM	Lost	1150	1230.2	1282.2	111.50	104.23
RAJA A.	PERAMBALUR(SC)	Won	1250	1165	1049.9	83.99	90.12
KRISHNAN C.	POLLACHI(SC)	Won	1150	1173	1118.5	97.26	95.35
THIRUNAVUKARASU	PUDUKKOTTAI	Not Cont	1150	1305.6	1174.6	102.14	89.97
MALAISAMY K.	RAMANATHAPURAM	Not Cont	1150	1154.2	1213.2	105.50	105.11
SAROJA V.	RASIPURAM(SC)	Not Cont	1100	1098	1041.5	94.68	94.85
SELVAGANAPATHI T.M.	SALEM	Not Cont	950	854	740.7	77.97	86.73
SUDARSANA NATCHIAPPAN B.M.	SIVAGANGA	Not Cont	1150	1205.4	734.1	63.83	60.90
VAIKO	SIVAKASI	Not Cont	1050	999.1	1065.6	101.49	106.66
KRISHNASWAMY A.	SRIPERUMBUDUR(SC)	Won	1250	1148.8	999	79.92	86.96
MURUGESAN S.	TENKASI(SC)	Lost	1250	1324.1	1343.7	107.50	101.48
PALANIMANICKAM S.S.	THANJAVUR	Won	1250	1266.6	1166.6	93.33	92.10

RAMACHANDRAN N. GINGEE	TINDIVANAM	Not Cont	1050	1052.3	1247.4	118.80	118.54
JAYASEELAN A.D.K.	TIRUCHENDUR	Not Cont	1250	1271.9	1339.2	107.14	105.29
KANNAPPAN M.	TIRUCHENGODE	Not Cont	1000	886.2	928.5	92.85	104.77
THALITH EZLILMALAI	TIRUCHIRAPALLI	Not Cont	1150	1302.7	1223.4	106.38	93.91
PANDIAN P.H.	TIRUNELVELI	Not Cont	1250	1318.2	1329.5	106.36	100.86
VENUGOPAL D.	TIRUPPATTUR	Won	1150	1153	1169.2	101.67	101.41
DURAI M.	VANDAVASI	Not Cont	1200	1249.3	1169.3	97.44	93.60
SHANMUGAM N.T.	VELLORE	Not Cont	1150	1107.9	1135.1	98.70	102.46
Tripura							
BAJU BAN RIYAN	TRIPURA EAST(ST)	won	1300	1407.6	976.4	75.11	69.37
KHAGEN DAS	TRIPURA WEST	won	1250	1200.1	1088.6	87.09	90.71
Uttar Pradesh							
RAJ BABBAR	AGRA	won	1100	1168.3	1201.6	109.24	102.85
TRIBHUWAN DATT	AKBARPUR(SC)	Not Cont	1250	1190.5	1145.4	91.63	96.21
SHEELA GAUTAM	ALIGARH	Lost	1100	1124	1036.9	94.26	92.25
MURLI MONOHAR JOSHI	ALLAHABAD	Lost	1050	957	797.6	75.96	83.34
SONIA GANDHI	AMETHI	Won	1200	1142.1	926.2	77.18	81.10
RASHID ALVI	AMROHA	Not Cont	950	962.8	923.9	97.25	95.96
KUNWAR SARVRAJ SINGH	AONLA	Won	1150	1246.7	1043.4	90.73	83.69
RAMA KANT YADAV	AZAMGARH	Won	1200	1192	1028.1	85.68	86.25
AJIT SINGH	BAGHPAT	Won	1200	1203	1156.5	96.38	96.13
PADMSEN CHAUDHARY	BAHRAICH	Lost	1150	1085.9	967.4	84.12	89.09

CHANDRA SHEKHAR	BALLIA	Won	1150	1058.5	941.1	81.83	88.91
RIZWAN ZAHEER ALIAS RIJJU BHAIYA	BALRAMPUR	Lost	1100	1090.6	1076.7	97.88	98.73
RAJ NARAIN PASHI	BANASGAON(SC)	Lost	1200	1134.5	1031.4	85.95	90.91
RAM SAJIWAN	BANDA	Lost	1200	1105.7	698.2	58.18	63.15
RAM SAGAR	BARABANKI(SC)	Lost	1150	1152.1	1117.9	97.21	97.03
SANTOSH KUMAR GANGWAR	BAREILLY	Won	1150	1111.7	1010.3	87.85	90.88
SHRI RAM CHAUHAN	BASTI(SC)	Lost	1150	1135	1006.9	87.56	88.71
SHEESHRAM SINGH RAVI	BIJNOR(SC)	Lost	1200	1117.1	1024.3	85.36	91.69
SHYAM BIHARI MISHRA	BILHAUR	Lost	1200	1141.8	905.2	75.43	79.28
SALEEM IQBAL SHERVANI	BUDAUN	Won	1150	1064	896.2	77.93	84.23
CHHATRA PAL	BULANDSHAHR	Not Cont	1200	1126	1060.2	88.35	94.16
SURESH PASI	CHAIL(SC)	Not Cont	1150	1162.9	1006.9	87.56	86.59
JAWAHAR LAL JAISWAL	CHANDAULI	Not Cont	1150	1058.3	952.6	82.83	90.01
SHRI PRAKASH MANI	DEORIA	Lost	1150	1155	936	81.39	81.04
RAM PAL SINGH	DOMARIAGANJ	Lost	1150	1155	1017.4	88.47	88.09
DEVENDRA SINGH YADAV	ETAH	Won	1150	1115	1078	93.74	96.68
RAGHURAJ SINGH SHAKYA	ETAWAH	Won	1150	1106	1011.5	87.96	91.46
VINAY KATIYAR	FAIZABAD	Not Cont	1100	1069.2	1044.2	94.93	97.66
CHANDRA BHUSHAN SINGH (MUNNOO BABU)	FARRUKHABAD	Won	1100	1107.5	1000.3	90.94	90.32
ASHOK PATEL	FATEHPUR	Lost	1200	1134.1	1055.5	87.96	93.07
RAM JILAL SUMAN	FIROZABAD(SC)	Won	1100	1072.9	1018.9	92.63	94.97
PYARE LAL SANKHWAR	GHATAMPUR(SC)	Lost	1200	1163.8	1009.4	84.12	86.73

MANOJ	GHAZIPUR	Lost	1200	1196.9	996	83.00	83.21
BAL KRISHNA	GHOSI	Not Cont	1100	1053	1041.1	94.65	98.87
BRAJ BHUSHAN SHARAN SINGH	GONDA	Not Cont	1100	1034.6	1131.7	102.88	109.39
ADITYA NATH	GORAKHPUR	Won	1150	1080.8	1002.7	87.19	92.77
ASHOK KUMAR SINGH CHANDEL	HAMIRPUR	Lost	1150	1092	1006.1	87.49	92.13
RAMESH CHAND TOMAR	HAPUR	Lost	1050	1002.5	790	75.24	78.80
JAI PRAKASH	HARDOI (SC)	Not Cont	1200	1131	1061.7	88.48	93.87
KISHAN LAL DILER	HATHRAS (SC)	Won	1100	1102.4	1073.1	97.55	97.34
BRIJLAL KHABRI	JALAUN(SC)	Lost	1200	1080	1093.1	91.09	101.21
PROFESSOR S.P. SINGH BAGHEL	JALESAR	Won	1200	1131.8	1057.8	88.15	93.46
CHINMAYANAND	JAUNPUR	Lost	1150	1023.6	731.4	63.60	71.45
SUJAN SINGH BUNDELA	JHANSI	Not Cont	800	804.1	812.6	101.58	101.06
AMIR ALAM	KAIRANA	Not Cont	1100	1094.3	1126.3	102.39	102.92
BENI PRASAD VERMA	KAISERGANJ	Won	1200	1128.4	1042.5	86.88	92.39
AKHILESH YADAV	KANNAUJ	Won	1150	1141	1058.7	92.06	92.79
SHRIPRAKASH JAISWAL	KANPUR	Won	1150	1156.9	1083.8	94.24	93.68
BHAL CHANDRA YADAV	KHALILABAD	Won	1200	1254.3	1058	88.17	84.35
RAVI PRAKASH VERMA	KHIRI/LAKHIMPUR	Won	1100	1050.5	952	86.55	90.62
ASHOK KUMAR PRADHAN	KHURJA(SC)	Won	1200	1171.2	998.4	83.20	85.25
ATAL BEHARI VAJPAYEE	LUCKNOW	Won	1150	1310.7	1201	104.43	91.63
CHANDRA NATH SINGH	MACHHLISHAHR	Lost	1150	1072.9	913.2	79.41	85.12
AKHILESH SINGH	MAHARAJGANJ	Lost	1100	1084.3	985.1	89.55	90.85

BALRAM SINGH YADAV	MAINPURI	Lost	1100	1062.2	910.1	82.74	85.68
CH. TEJVIR SINGH	MATHURA	Lost	1100	1166.7	1127.5	102.50	96.64
AVTAR SINGH BHADANA	MEERUT	Not Cont	1150	1187.9	1081.7	94.06	91.06
RAM RATI BIND	MIRZAPUR	Not Cont	1000	986.9	698	69.80	70.73
SUSHILA SAROJ	MISRIKH(SC)	Lost	1100	1170.2	1106.7	100.61	94.57
REENA CHAUDHARY	MOHANLALGANJ(SC)	Lost	1050	1023.9	1101.3	104.89	107.56
SAIDUZZAMAN	MUZAFFARNAGAR	Lost	1100	1064.6	1050.5	95.50	98.68
RAM NAGINA MISHRA	PADRAUNA	Lost	1050	1010	958.6	91.30	94.91
DHARAMRAJ SINGH PATEL	PHULPUR	Not Cont	1200	1136.8	979.6	81.63	86.17
MANEKA GANDHI	PILIBHIT	Won	1050	967.8	982.4	93.56	101.51
RAJKUMARI RATNA SINGH	PRATAPGARH	Lost	1150	1080.9	970.1	84.36	89.75
CAPTAIN SATISH SHARMA	RAE BARELI	Not Cont	900	917.5	821.7	91.30	89.56
BEGUM NOOR BANO URF MAHTAB ZAMANI BEGUM	RAMPUR	Lost	1100	1047.3	1170.7	106.43	111.78
RAM SHAKAL	ROBERTSGANJ(SC)	Lost	1200	1195.2	1079.1	89.93	90.29
MANSOOR ALI KHAN	SAHARANPUR	Lost	1100	1197.1	1196.8	108.80	99.97
TUFANI SAROJ	SAIDPUR(SC)	Won	1250	1351.6	1022.5	81.80	75.65
BABBAN RAJBHAR	SALEMPUR	Not Cont	1200	1205.8	919	76.58	76.21
MULAYAM SINGH YADAV	SAMBHAL	Not Cont	1200	1172	1006	83.83	85.84
DAUD AHMAD	SHAHABAD	Not Cont	1200	1192	825.9	68.83	69.29
RAMAMURTHI SINGH VERMA	SHAHJAHANPUR	Lost	1200	1086	1026.8	85.57	94.55
RAJESH VERMA	SITAPUR	Won	1100	1185.7	1120.5	101.86	94.50
JAI BHADRA SINGH	SULTANPUR	Not Cont	1150	1099.5	839.1	72.97	76.32

DEEPAK KUMAR	UNNAO	Lost	1150	1226	1047.4	91.08	85.43
SHANKAR PRASAD JAISWAL	VARANASI	Lost	1050	1022.3	948.4	90.32	92.77
CHANDRA VIJAY SINGH ALIAS BABYRAJA	MORADABAD	Lost	1200	1178.2	1083.1	90.26	91.93
BALIRAM	LALGANJ (SC)	Lost	1200	1185.5	934.4	77.87	78.82
West Bengal							
JOACHIM BAXLA	ALIPURDUARS(ST)	Won	650	606.4	339.5	52.23	55.99
ANIL BASU	ARAMBAGH	Won	1150	1106	737.6	64.14	66.69
BIKASH CHOWDHURY	ASANSOL	Won	600	528	359	59.83	67.99
BARMAN RANEN	BALURGHAT(SC)	Won	800	754.9	415.3	51.91	55.01
ACHARIA BASUDEB	BANKURA	Won	1150	1180.4	1035.6	90.05	87.73
RANJIT KUMAR PANJA	BARASAT	Lost	1100	1073.9	818.6	74.42	76.23
TARIT BARAN TOPDAR	BARRACKPORE	Won	550	508	491.2	89.31	96.69
AJOY CHAKRABORTY	BASIRHAT	Won	800	819.3	631.7	78.96	77.10
ADHIR RANJAN CHOWDHURY	BEHRAMPORE	Won	1300	1327	1049.3	80.72	79.07
RAM CHANDRA DOME	BIRBHUM(SC)	Won	1100	1086	941	85.55	86.65
SOMNATH CHATTERJEE	BOLPUR	Won	1100	1125.3	869.7	79.06	77.29
SAR NIKHILANANDA	BURDWAN	Won	800	816	587	73.38	71.94
AJIT KUMAR PANJA	CALCUTTA N.E	Lost	1200	1432.4	1547.8	128.98	108.06
SUDIP BANDYOPADHYAY	CALCUTTA N.W	Lost	1050	1121.3	1233.3	117.46	109.99
MAMATA BANERJEE	CALCUTTA SOUTH	Won	1200	1276.5	523.5	43.63	41.01
NITISH SENGUPTA	CONTAI	Lost	1100	1090	989.4	89.95	90.77
AMAR ROY PRADHAN	COOCH BEHAR(SC)	Lost	1150	1126.3	609.6	53.01	54.12

S.P. LEPCHA	DARJEELING	Not Cont	1200	1176.8	1065.4	88.78	90.53
SAMIK LAHIRI	DIAMOND HARBOUR	Won	1000	1076.3	506.3	50.63	47.04
TAPAN SIKDAR	DUM DUM	Lost	950	875.3	754.3	79.40	86.18
SUNIL KHAN	DURGAPUR (SC)	Won	900	896	771	85.67	86.05
RUPCHAND PAL	HOOGHLY	Won	1150	1179	565.5	49.17	47.96
SWADESH CHAKRABORTY	HOWRAH	Won	1250	1253.6	622	49.76	49.62
KRISHNA BOSE	JADAVPUR	Lost	1050	1057.6	318.9	30.37	30.15
MINATI SEN	JALPAIGURI	Won	1000	1020.8	473.1	47.31	46.35
ABUL HASNAT KHAN	JANGIPUR	Not Cont	1150	1127.3	960	83.48	85.16
RUPCHAND MURMU	JHARGRAM(ST)	Won	1200	1301	1097	91.42	84.32
SANAT KUMAR MANDAL	JOYNAGAR(SC)	Won	1100	1088.9	528.9	48.08	48.57
MAHBOOB ZAHEDI	KATWA	Won	900	829	619.4	68.82	74.72
SATYABRATA MOOKHERJEE	KRISHNAGAR	Lost	1250	1359.9	1012.1	80.97	74.42
A. B. A. GHANI KHAN CHOUDHARY	MALDA	Won	1150	1263	1112	96.70	88.04
RADHIKA RANJAN PRAMANIK	MATHURAPUR(SC)	Not Cont	900	914.8	290.8	32.31	31.79
PRABODH PANDA	MIDNAPORE	Won	1200	1195	1125.1	93.76	94.15
MOINUL HASSAN AHMAD	MURSHIDABAD	Not Cont	1200	1134.3	972.1	81.01	85.70
ALAKESH DAS	NABADWIP(SC)	Won	1250	1212	956.8	76.54	78.94
BIKRAM SARKAR	PANSKURA	Not Cont	1200	1184.8	1022.7	85.23	86.32
BIRSINGH MAHATO	PURULIA	Won	1100	950.5	1090.8	99.16	114.76
PRIYA RANJAN DASMUNSI	RAIGANJ	Won	1150	1155	962.3	83.68	83.32
AKBOR ALI KHANDOKER	SERAMPORE	Lost	1200	1178.9	550.5	45.88	46.70

LAKSHMAN CHANDRA SETH	TAMLUK	Won	1150	1106	1063.5	92.48	96.16
HANNAN MOLLAH	ULUBERIA	Won	1150	1154.5	886.4	77.08	76.78
SANDHYA BAURI	VISHNUPUR(SC)	Not Cont	1200	1168	1011.9	84.33	86.64
Andaman & Nicobar Islands							
BISHNU PADA RAY	ANDAMAN & NICOBAR ISLANDS	Lost	1100	1181.2	1216.3	110.57	102.97
Chandigarh							
PAWAN KUMAR BANSAL	CHANDIGARH	won	950	964	1088.9	114.62	112.96
D&N Havveli							
DELKAR MOHANBHAI SANJIBHAI		won	1150	1252.5	1217.2	105.84	97.18
Daman & Dau							
PATEL DAHYABHAI VALLABHBHAI		Won	1150	1127	1213.2	105.50	107.65
Delhi							
MADAN LAL KHURANA	DELHI SADAR	Not Cont	1050	1053.8	886.9	84.47	84.16
LAL BIHARI TIWARI	EAST DELHI	Lost	900	838.3	748.6	83.18	89.30
ANITA ARYA	KAROL BAGH(SC)	Lost	1100	1158.7	974.5	88.59	84.10
JAGMOHAN	NEW DELHI	Lost	1000	952.1	800.5	80.05	84.08
SAHIB SINGH VERMA	OUTER DELHI	Lost	900	822.6	879.4	97.71	106.90
VIJAY KUMAR MALHOTRA	SOUTH DELHI	won	1050	979.1	839.2	79.92	85.71
VIJAY GOEL	CHANDINI CHOWK	Not Cont	850	833.9	689.1	81.07	82.64
Lakshadweep							
P.M. SAYEED	LAKSHADWEEP(ST)	Lost	1050	1039	850.7	81.02	81.88

Pondichery							
M O H FAROOK	PONDICHERRY	Not Cont	1150	1200.4	1106.6	96.23	92.19
Chhatishgarg							
BALIRAM KASHYAP	BASTAR(ST)	won	1150	1241.4	1186.8	103.20	95.60
PUNNULAL MOHLE	BILASPUR(SC)	won	900	803	782.6	86.96	97.46
TARACHAND SAHU	DURG	won	1100	1168.8	1126.1	102.37	96.35
CHARANDAS MAHANT	JANJGIR	Lost	1050	1029.5	1096.6	104.44	106.52
SOHAN POTAI	KANKER(ST)	won	1200	1200.1	1185.5	98.79	98.78
SHYAMA CHARAN SHUKLA	MAHASAMUND	Not Cont	1050	1009.2	963.1	91.72	95.43
VISHNUDEO SAI	RAIGARH(ST)	won	1150	1123	1044.2	90.80	92.98
RAMESH BAIS	RAIPUR	won	1100	1039.4	810.1	73.65	77.94
RAMAN SINGH	RAJNANDGAON	Not Cont	900	879.4	799.4	88.82	90.90
P.R. KHUTE	SARANGARH(SC)	Not Cont	1050	1004.2	984.9	93.80	98.08
KHEL SAI SINGH	SARGUJA(ST)	Lost	1100	1151.4	1132.8	102.98	98.38
Uttaranchal							
BACHI SINGH RAWAT	ALMORA	won	1150	1106.8	1110.4	96.56	100.33
GEN.(RTD) BHUWAN CHANDRA KHANDUR	GARHWAL	won	1050	1025.1	900.6	85.77	87.85
HARPAL SINGH SATHI	HARDWAR(SC)	Lost	1150	1221.2	1115.5	97.00	91.34
MAHENDRA SINGH PAL	NAINITAL	Not Cont	1150	1183.5	1068.7	92.93	90.30
MANABENDRA SHAH	TEHRI GARHWAL	won	1050	986.9	1071.3	102.03	108.55
Jharkhand							
NAGMANI	CHATRA	Lost	1100	1025.8	865.8	78.71	84.40

RITA VERMA	DHANBAD	Lost	700	656.8	631.5	90.21	96.15
SHIBU SOREN	DUMKA(ST)	won	700	710.7	578	82.57	81.33
RABINDRA KUMAR PANDEY	GIRIDIH	Lost	1150	1122.6	990.1	86.10	88.20
PRADEEP YADAV	GODDA	Lost	1200	1170.1	1140.1	95.01	97.44
YASHWANT SINHA	HAZARIBAGH	Lost	1150	1272.7	800.5	69.61	62.90
ABHA MAHATO	JAMSHEDPUR	Lost	1050	1016.8	1044	99.43	102.68
KARIYA MUNDA	KHUNTI(ST)	Lost	1200	1157	610.7	50.89	52.78
TILAKDHARI PD SINGH	KODARMA	Lost	1100	894.3	801.2	72.84	89.59
DUKHA BHAGAT	LOHARDAGA(ST)	Lost	1000	1023.1	739.7	73.97	72.30
BRAJ MOHAN RAM	PALAMAU(SC)	Lost	1100	1014.9	931.3	84.66	91.76
THOMAS HANSDA	RAJMAHAL(ST)	Lost	1100	963.3	662.3	60.21	68.75
RAMTAHAL CHOUDHARY	RANCHI	Lost	1100	1098.4	902.3	82.03	82.15
LAXMAN GILUWA	SINGHBHUM(ST)	Lost	1150	1129.9	974.7	84.76	86.26

Abbreviations

AIDMK	All India Dravida Munnetra Kazhagam
AITC	All India Trinamool Congress
BDO	Block Development Officer
BJD	Biju Janta Dal
BJP	Bharatiya Janata Party
BSF	Border Security Force
BSP	Bahujan Samaj Party
CAG	Comptroller and Auditor General of India
CEO	Chief Executive Officer
CISF	Central Industrial Security Force
CJI	Chief Justice of India
CM	Chief Minister
CPI	Communist Party of India
CPI(M)/CPM	Communist Party of India (Marxist)
CRPF	Central Reserve Police Force
DC	District Collector/Deputy Commissioner
DFAD	Department of Foreign Aid and Development
DM	District Magistrate
DMK	Dravida Munnetra Kazhagam
DPI	Department of Programme Implementation
DPR	Detailed Project Report

Dy PM	Deputy Prime Minister
ET	Economic Times
EVM	Electronic Voting Machine
FBL	All India Forward Block
FC	Finance Commission
FPM	Federal Party of Manipur
HP	Himachal Pradesh
HT	Hindustan Times
HVC	Himachal Vikas Congress
IFAD	International Fund for Agriculture Development
IFDP	Indian Federal Democratic Party
INC	Indian National Congress
Ind.	Independent
INLD	Indian National Lok Dal
J&K	Jammu & Kashmir
JD (U)/ JDU	Janata Dal (United)
JKNC	Jammu & Kashmir National Conference
LF	Left Front
LFA	Logical Framework Analysis
LJP	Lok Janshakti Party
LS	Lok Sabha
MCC	Maoist Communist Centre
MDMK	Marumalarchi Dravida Munnetra Kazhagam
MLA	Member of Legislative Assembly
MLALADS	Member of Legislative Assembly Local Area Development Scheme
MLKSC	Muslim League Kerala State Committee
MNF	Mizo National Front
MOV	Means Of Verification
MP	Member of Parliament
MPLADS	Member of Parliament Local Area Development Scheme

MPP	Manipur People's Party
MSCP	Manipur State Congress Party
MW	Mega Watt
NCP	Nationalist Congress Party
ND	New Delhi
NDA	National Democratic Alliance
NDC	National Development Council
NDTV	New Delhi Telelvision
NGO	Non-Governmental Organisation
OTH	Others
OVI	Objectively Verifiable Indicators
PDP	Peoples Democratic Party
PEO	Programme Evaluation Organisation
PHED	Public Health & Engineering Department
PM	Prime Minister
POTA	Prevention of Terrorism Act
PRA	Participatory Rural Appraisal
PRI	Panchayati Raj Institution
PW	Pepole's War
RJD	Rashtriya Janata Dal
RJP	Rashtriya Janata Party
RLD	Rashtriya Lok Dal
RPA	Representation of Peoples Act
RPI	Republican Party of India
RS	Rajya Sabha
SAD	Shiromani Akali Dal
SAP	Samata Party
SC	Scheduled Caste
SHG	Self Help Group
SJP(R)	Samajwadi Janata Party (Rashtriya)
SP	Samajwadi Party
SS	Shiv Sena
ST	Scheduled Tribe

TDP	Telgu Desam Party
TIE	The Indian Express
TN	Tamil Nadu
TOI	Times of India
TRS	Telengana Rastra Samiti
TV	Television
UP	Uttar Pradesh
UPA	United Progressive Alliance
UT	Union Territory
VLW	Village Level Worker
WB	West Bengal

References

Bagchi, Amaresh. (2000), "A Note of Observations on the Need to Strengthen the Equalising Role of Fiscal Transfers", *Report of the Eleventh Finance Commission (For 2000-2005).*

Chambers, Robert. (1997), *Whose Reality Counts? Putting the first last*, Intermediate Technology Publications, London.

CIDA, Guide for the use of the Logical Framework Approach in the Management and Evaluation of CIDA's Integrated Development Projects.

Coleman, G. (1987), "Project Planning: Logical Framework Approach to the Monitoring and Evaluation of Agricultural and Rural Development Projects", *Project Appraisal*, Beech Tree Publishing, Surrey, England, Vol-2, No-4, Page 251-259.

Comptroller and Auditor General of India (2001), *Report of the CAG of India for the year ended March 2000: Member of Parliament Local Area Development Scheme, Union Government (Civil), Performance Appriasal, No. 3A of 2001.*

Dreze, Jean. and Sen, Amartya. (1996), *India: Economic Development and Social Opportunity*, Oxford University Press, Delhi.

GOI (1998), *Manual on Community Needs Assessment Approach (formerly Target Free Approach) in Family Welfare Programme*, Department of Family Welfare, Ministry of Health and Family Welfare, New Delhi.

GOI (2003), *Development Evaluation in India, Contemporary Issues and Approaches: Report Submitted by the Core Group Constituted by the Comptroller and Auditor General of India.*

GOI (2003), *Statistical Handbook, updated upto : Winter Session (Part-II)*, Ministry of Parliamentary Affairs, New Delhi.

GTZ (1988), *ZOOP (an introduction to the method)*, Deutsche Gesellschaft fur Technische Zusammenarbeit (GZT) GmbH, Postfach 5180, D-6232 Eschborn 1 bei, Frankfurt am Main, Germany.

IFAD, *Managing for Impact in Rural Development: A Guide for Project Monitoring and Evaluation.*

Kumar, Somesh. (2002), *Methods for Community Participation: A Complete Guide for Practitioners*, Vistaar Publications, New Delhi.

Lok Sabha Secretariat (2001), *The Constitution of India (As modified up to 1st January, 2001)*, New Delhi.

Mohanty, Siba Sankar. (2004), *Rhetoric and Reality of MPLADS*, Centre for Budget and Governance Accountability, New Delhi.

Mosse, David. (1998), "Process Documentation Research and Process Monitoring: Cases and Issues", in David Mosse, John Farrington and Alan Rew edited, *Development as Process: Concepts and methods for working with complexity*, Routledge, London.

PCI (1979), *Project Management Systems (PMS): An Integrated System Approach to the Project Cycle, Washington DC.*

Planning Commission (2001), *Indian Planning Experience: A Statistical Profile*, Government of India, New Delhi.

Planning Commission (2002), *Five Year Plan: 2002-2007, Volume-I, Dimensions and Strategies*, New Delhi.

Planning Commission (2003), "Follow-up Action on PEO Study: The Case of Member of Parliament Local Area Development Scheme (MPLADS)", in *Development Evaluation in PEO and Its Impact*, Programme Evaluation Organisation, New Delhi.

Planning Commission (2003), *Development Evaluation in PEO and Its Impact*, Programme Evaluation Organisation, New Delhi.

PRAXIS (1998), *Participatory Monitoring and Evaluation: An Introductory Pack* (Originally compiled by Institute of

Development Studies, University of Sussex, 1997), New Delhi.

Programme Evaluation Organisation (2001), *Evaluation Report on Member of Parliament Local Area Development Scheme*, Planning Commission, New Delhi.

Puri, H. K. (1995), "Federalism in a Multi-cultural Society", in M. P. Singh and H. Ray edited *Indian Political System*, Jnanada Prakashan (P&P), New Delhi.

Report of the Eleventh Finance Commission (For 2000-2005), June, 2000.

Report of the Twelfth Finance Commission (2005-10), November, 2004.

Riker, William H. (1988), *Liberalism against Populism: A Confrontation between the Theory of Democracy and the Theory of Social Choice*, Waveland Press, Inc. 2nd Edition.

Roy, Meenu. (2000), *Electoral Politics in India: Election Process and Outcomes, Voting Behavior and Current Trends*, Deep & Deep Publications Pvt. Ltd, New Delhi.

Saxena, Rekha. (1999), "Indian Federalism at the Crossroads", in *Essays on Indian Government and Politics: A Continuing Review*, Jawahar Publishers and Distributors, New Delhi, Page 119-150.

Sen, Amartya. (2004), "Development as Freedom: An Indian Perspective", extracts from the speech at a seminar organized by the FICCI, *Hard News*.

Singh, M.P. (1995), "Federalism: Constitution and Dynamics" in M. P. Singh and H. Ray edited *Indian Political System*, Jnanada Prakashan (P&P), New Delhi.

Index